W9-BHK-961

The New
China

The New
CHINA

BY JEFFREY H. HACKER

A GROLIER COMPANY

FRANKLIN WATTS 1986
NEW YORK LONDON TORONTO SYDNEY
AN IMPACT BOOK

Map by Vantage Art, Inc.

Photographs courtesy of:
Eastfoto: pp. 6, 27, 30, 36, 44,
53, 74; The Bettmann Archive: p. 10;
AP/Wide World: p. 13, 38;
UPI/Bettmann Newsphotos: pp. 15,
19, 61; the author: pp.
49, 57, 68, 110.

Library of Congress Cataloging in Publication Data
Hacker, Jeffrey H.
The new China.
(An Impact book)
Bibliography: p.
Includes index.
Summary: Discusses the history of the People's
Republic of China with emphasis on the changes in
attitudes, politics, and day-to-day life.
1. China—History—1949–   . [1. China—History—
1949–   ] I. Title.
DS777.55.H24   1986   951.05   85-29414
ISBN 0-531-10156-8

Contents

FOR THE
HACKERS,
SHENASSAS,
AND
WOLFFS

Chapter 1
The Middle Kingdom

Since the journey of Marco Polo in the thirteenth century, China has been a source of great fascination—
and foreboding—to the Western world. The Italian
adventurer brought back wondrous tales of an ancient
and alien culture, a land of towering pagodas, green
jade, great emperors, and unheard of religions. Not all
Europeans believed Polo's accounts of old Cathay, but
many were quite enthralled and perhaps a little dis-
quieted. Over the centuries, as merchants and mis-
sionaries verified Polo's descriptions, Western fears
seemed to grow. Here was a vast new world of strange
people and bizarre customs. If only because it was so
remote, so isolated, and so formidable, China came to
be regarded as a "sleeping giant." Five hundred years
after Marco Polo's journey, Napoleon Bonaparte pre-
dicted: "When China rises, the world will tremble."

The world today hardly trembles at the thought of
China, but the fascination and wonderment persist.
The Chinese civilization is the oldest in the world,
traceable to more than 4,000 years ago. Its rich traditions in art, music, literature, science, and medicine
remain very much alive. Despite the best efforts of
modern political leaders, the rituals and folk customs
of ancient China are still in evidence. Mao Tse-tung,

THE PEOPLE'S REPUBLIC OF CHINA

U.S.S.R.

U.S.S.R.

MONGOLIA

TARIM HE
(Tarim River)

XINJIANG
(Sinkiang)

GANSU
(Kansu)

PAKISTAN

QINGHAI
(Tsinghai)

XIZANG
(Tibet)

NU JIANG
(Salween River)

LANCANG JIANG
(Mekong River)

INDIA

SICHUAN
(Szechwan)

YARLUNG ZANGBO JIANG
(Brahmaputra River)

Lhasa ●
(Lhasa)

NEPAL

INDIA

BHUTAN

YUNNAN
(Yunnan)

INDIA

kilometers

0 100 200 300 400 500

0   100   200   300   400   500

miles

BANGLADESH

BURMA

VIET-
NAM

LAOS

Boundary representations are
not necessarily authoritative

U.S.S.R.

HEILONG JIANG (Amur River)

HEILONGJIANG
(Heilungkiang)

NEI MONGGOL
(Inner Mongolia)

JILIN
(Kirin)

LIAONING
(Liaoning)

YALU JIANG
(Yalu River)

N.
KOREA

HUANG HO
(Ye ow R ver)

HEBEI
(Hopeh)

Beijing
(Peking)

Tianjin
(Tientsin)

S. KOREA

INGXIA
(ingsia)

SHANXI
(Shansi)

SHANDONG
(Shantung)

Yellow Sea

East
China
Sea

Xian
(Sian)

HENAN
(Honan)

JIANGSU
(Kiangsu)

SHANGHAI
(Shanghai)

SHAANXI
(Shensi)

Nanjing
(Nanking)

ANHUI
(Anhwei)

CHANG JIANG
(Yangtze River)

HUBEI
(Hupeh)

ZHEJIANG
(Chekiang)

Province-level Names		
Pinyin (Officially adopted 1/1/79)	ANHUI	
Previous Romanization (Wade–Giles)	(Anhwei)	

UIZHOU
(Kweichow)

HUNAN
(Hunan)

JIANGXI
(Kiangsi)

FUJIAN
(Fukien)

TAIWAN

GUANGXI
(Kwangsi)

GUANGDONG
(Kwangtung)

Guangzhou
(Canton)

HONG KONG
MACAO

South
China

Sea

HAINAN

the Communist revolution, and a regime that shut out foreigners for a quarter of a century created new mysteries. And finally, a population that now exceeds *one billion* has added to the awe and fascination of the West: What is life like for a quarter of the world's people? How are things changing? How does China view the outside world? Will the People's Republic join the United States, Japan, Western Europe, and the Soviet Union as a major economic power? Will East and West ever really meet?

WALLS

The visitor to China today feels a little like Marco Polo, overwhelmed by new sights, sounds, smells, and tastes. The first impression is often the sheer masses of people. In Chinese cities, floods of humanity overflow the sidewalks into the streets. Waves of bicycles rush by, bells jingling. Old men with wispy beards, women carrying live chickens from market, factory workers wearing Mao jackets, rosy-cheeked children wearing brightly colored smocks all turn and stare. The Chinese are still unaccustomed to seeing Westerners. Their stares imply no threat, just curiosity.

Another impression the foreigner has soon after arriving in China is the abundance of walls. They seem to be everywhere—garden walls, village walls, temple walls, walls along the street, walls around official buildings. Traditional Chinese homes were surrounded by high walls; today's residential complexes are similarly hidden from view. Whole cities, such as Peking and Nanking*, once were protected by heavily fortified

---

* In this book, Chinese names and places generally follow the new *pinyin* system of English spelling. Since 1979, *pinyin* has been the official English transliteration system of the People's Republic. How-

4

barriers and ramparts. Peking, in fact, had walls inside walls: the Forbidden City, the sprawling residence of the emperor, was surrounded by a wide moat and walls 35 feet (11 m) high. And then, of course, there is the Great Wall. Winding 3,000 miles (4,828 km) across northern China, it was begun 2,500 years ago to keep out invaders.

There could be no better symbol for China than the Great Wall. It is, first of all, an engineering and construction wonder, a monument to the inventiveness, industriousness, and great achievements of Chinese civilization. Built stone by stone across mountains and desert, it also embodies the deeply ingrained Chinese spirit of communal endeavor and group cooperation. And finally, the Great Wall suggests a society insulated from the outside world and leery of other peoples. One has the sense that the Great Wall was built as much to keep China in as to keep barbarians out.

The many other walls throughout the country make plain that the Chinese are an intensely private people, at least when it comes to family life. As it has for centuries, the family unit remains the foundation of Chinese society and culture. Extended families— children, parents, grandparents, aunts, and uncles— often live under the same roof or in connected quarters. With China's vast population, walls help preserve the privacy of the family.

---

ever, many proper names will be more familiar to readers in their traditional (Wade-Giles) form. In those cases, the older spellings will be used. Peking and Nanking are the traditional spellings; in *pinyin* they are Beijing and Nanjing. Other proper names for which the old spelling will be retained are: Canton (not Guangzhou), Chiang Ching-kuo (not Jiang Jingguo), Chiang Kai-shek (not Jiang Jieshi), Chou En-lai (not Zhou Enlai), Confucius (not Kong Fuzi), Kuomintang (not Guomindang), Mao Tse-tung (not Mao Zedong), Quemoy (not Jinmen), Tientsin (not Tianjin), Yangtze (not Changjiang).

A section of the Great Wall near Peking.
The Great Wall is a symbol of the
ancient civilization of China.

At the national level, the Chinese have long demonstrated a similar need for privacy, insulation, and strong internal identification. China has been, in a sense, a civilization behind walls. It has worked to feed its millions, suffered great natural disasters, and contended with conflicting forces both inside and outside its borders. There is great pride in Chinese history and a profound spirit of nationalism. There has also been a deep and long-standing xenophobia—a fear of anything foreign. The Great Wall is only a symbol of this proud and fearful isolationism; the evidence is seen throughout the political life of the nation. The reasons for it are part geographic and part cultural. It is also rooted in a history of invasion and oppression by the outside world.

LEGACIES

China's name in the language of its people is *Zhong Guo*—"The Middle Kingdom." The ancient Chinese viewed their civilization as the center of the known world Theirs was the most advanced culture and noblest empire. Outsiders were barbarians. The Chinese emperor was the "Son of Heaven," a divine ruler to whom all foreign visitors should pay tribute. The Chinese ideogram (picture symbol) for the country is a square with a slash through the center: 中 The shape of the character suggests China's stable perception of itself; the single line through the middle represents China's place at the center of the civilized world.

The name "China" most likely comes from the period in its history known as the Qin dynasty (221–206 B.C.). It was at this time, under the famous emperor Qin Shi Huang Di, that a large number of rival states were unified under a single empire. The ideal of a unified sovereign nation was to last more than

2,000 years, to the present day. Among the other accomplishments of Qin Shi Huang Di was to link the various sections of the Great Wall that had been built by individual states.

The next major period in Chinese history was the Han dynasty (206 B.C.–A.D. 220), a time of cultural growth and splendor. Paper and porcelain were invented, the first dictionary was compiled, and the imperial university became a center of scholarship and education. Traders and emissaries traveled across Central Asia along the Silk Road, bringing back knowledge of the Roman Empire and Hellenic world. To this day the Chinese refer to themselves as the Han people.

Perhaps the greatest legacy of the Han dynasty was the emergence of Confucianism as the official doctrine of the Chinese imperial state. Confucius, revered as the Supreme Sage and Foremost Thinker, had actually lived hundreds of years before (551–479 B.C.). It was shortly before the beginning of the Christian era, however, that his teachings were adopted as the state creed, and they remained so until the twentieth century. So overwhelming was the influence of that creed that if the Chinese way of life were to be characterized in one word it would be "Confucian." A philosophy and code of ethics rather than a religion, Confucianism is founded on the fundamental goodness and sanctity of humankind. At the core of the Confucian system is the principle of *jen*— the love, benevolence, or good-heartedness that is present in all humans. The Confucian ideal is the harmony of the individual and the well-ordered society, based on mutual moral obligations and five basic forms of human relations: between ruler and minister, father and son, elder brother and younger brother, husband and wife, and one friend and another. In this neatly structured ideal society, a ruler governs by moral principle; every family has its place beneath the ruler; and every individual has his place within the family. Filial piety and brotherly respect are the two fundamental virtues. It was a code of ethics and government that became the essential ideology ensuring the political unity of China for more than 2,000 years.

Other great and minor dynasties followed the Han. Some lasted only decades; others flourished for centuries. Advances were made in science, agriculture, and the arts. Confucianism was briefly discarded, then resurrected. The Buddhist religion took hold. China became the dominant force in East Asia—the great "Middle Kingdom," the center of the known world.

FOREIGN DEVILS

It was in the thirteenth century that the whole of China came under foreign rule for the first time. Mongol barbarians led by Genghis Khan poured in from the north early in the century and took over vast territories. Then in 1279, Kublai Khan completed the conquest of China and declared himself emperor. The Mongols established the Yuan dynasty, which lasted until 1368. During that period there was significant trade with the West via the Silk Road. There was a steady influx of foreigners (beginning with Marco Polo) bearing gifts for the emperor as well as new ideas. Christians and Muslims made the journey. Western science and technology came east. Chinese innovations—from the compass to gunpowder—went west.

The next foreigners to take over and rule China were invaders from Manchuria in the northeast. The Manchus conquered China and established the Qing dynasty in 1644. China's boundaries were extended, its population exploded, and the national culture

The Polo brothers, Venetians who traveled to China
in the 1200s, meeting with Kublai Khan.
Marco Polo became an emissary for the Khan
in China, India, and Southeast Asia.
Polo's accounts of his travels have
been useful to historians.

continued to flourish. In fact, Chinese ways had become so advanced and so deeply entrenched that the Manchus were gradually assimilated into the native culture rather than vice versa. The Qing dynasty lasted until 1911.

In the 1800s, meanwhile, China had suffered greatly at the hands of other "foreign devils." Since the seventeenth century, Europe had been conducting an increasing amount of trade with China, importing tea, silk, jade, and other goods. American merchants eventually joined in the China trade. The Chinese, however, remained characteristically leery of foreigners. In fact, the British and Americans were confined to a small area outside Canton, with severe restrictions on their activities. The British were anxious to expand their exports of opium and to gain access to other Chinese ports, but the emperor refused. The British responded by sending in gunboats and soldiers. The so-called Opium War broke out in 1839 and lasted three years. Shanghai and Nanking fell to the British, open trade was forced in five "treaty ports," and the Chinese were made to import vast amounts of opium. Britain also took possession of Hong Kong. For the Chinese it was a humiliating defeat that would not be forgotten for a very long time.

Severely weakened, the Qing suffered another disastrous defeat at the hands of Japan in 1894–1895, losing what is now Korea, Taiwan, and various island territories. The new defeat gave rise to strong anti-imperialist sentiments among the Chinese, which exploded in the Boxer Rebellion of 1899–1900. A secret society based in northern China, the Boxers led an armed rebellion against Russian, British, German, and French installations in various provinces. In Peking, their siege of the foreign quarter lasted fifty days, until an expeditionary force of seven Western nations and Japan put them to flight. With Peking in the hands of the foreigners, the Chinese were forced to accept a diplomatic settlement in 1901. The terms were harsh.

After the fall of the Qing dynasty in 1911, China became a constitutional republic for the first time in its long history. The first president was Dr. Sun Yat-sen. The new republic took part in World War I, primarily to regain a province that had been seized by Japan. But again it came away disappointed by the machinations of the West. At the Versailles Peace Conference, China was denied sovereignty over the province held by Japan. In fact, Japan was accorded special privileges in China.

After a decade-long struggle for control, Chiang Kai-shek emerged as the leader of the Chinese republic. He sought desperately to reestablish political unity, but he faced considerable opposition from within—as well as another foreign invasion, this time by Japan. By 1931 the Japanese had overrun Manchuria, by 1933 they had reached the outskirts of Peking, and by October 1938 they controlled the northern and eastern provinces of China. Only with its defeat in World War II did Japan withdraw its forces.

With so long a history of invasion and subjugation by "foreign devils," there was no small irony in the triumph of Communism—a system of government with European origins—in China in 1949. The Communist system had first been proposed by a German, Karl Marx; the country Marx had in mind for this new type

General and Madame Chiang Kai-shek in 1948. Chiang was the head of China's Nationalist government. He and his Nationalist forces were driven out of China by the Communists in 1949.

12

of government was Great Britain; and the first country actually to try the experiment was Russia. Now, under a revolutionary leader named Mao Tse-tung, a form of Communism would be adopted in Zhong Guo—the proud, xenophobic, long harassed "Middle Kingdom."

CHINA TODAY—
LAND AND PEOPLE

The People's Republic of China, stretching from central to eastern Asia, is the third largest nation in the world by total area, following the Soviet Union and Canada. At 3.7 million square miles (9.6 million sq km), it is slightly larger than the United States (3.62 million square miles or 9.4 million sq km). It is a vast country with great diversity in terrain and climate. To the west there are broad expanses of desert, towering mountain ranges, and high plateau lands. To the east, China has more than 4,000 miles (6,400 km) of coastline with many excellent harbors; the coast lies on the Yellow Sea in the north, the East China Sea in the center, and the South China Sea in the south. The Siberian steppes to the northeast are dry and frigid in winter. To the far south are lush jungles and a subtropical climate.

The most fundamental economic problems of China lie in its very geography. Fully two-thirds of its land is mountainous or desert; only about one-tenth can be cultivated. With a population of more than 1 billion, that comes to about one-fifth of an acre of agricultural land per person—barely enough for subsistence. Almost all of China's arable land lies in the eastern half of the country, which has some of the best-watered land in the world. Three great river systems—the 3,000-mile (4,800 km) Huang He (Yellow River), the nearly 4,000-mile (6,400 km) Yangtze (Long River),

A section of the Red Flag Irrigation Canal cut into the mountains of Honan Province. Before the building of the canal, the area was incapable of supporting agriculture.

and the 1,300-mile (2,080 km) Xijiang (West River)—provide water for vast farmlands in their fertile valleys and plains. A significant portion of China's population lives in these valleys and plains, and several major cities are sustained by the transportation, industrial, and hydroelectric capabilities of the three rivers. Indeed it was along the Yellow River that the Chinese civilization had its origins, and today this region remains the heart of the country in many ways.

The Yangtze, which flows west to east and empties into the East China Sea near the port city of Shanghai, is a natural dividing line between north and south China. While the demarcation is not geographically precise, it does separate two parts of China that differ in fundamental ways. The north tends to be arid and cold. Wheat is its major crop. The common language is basic Mandarin, and the culture is traditional Han Chinese. By contrast, the south tends to be humid and hot, with moist land suitable for growing rice and cotton. Because of the mixing of various ethnic groups, southern Chinese are somewhat different in appearance and temperament from northerners. They follow different customs and speak different dialects.

China is a land of great cities; at least two dozen major metropolitan areas have a population of more than one million. Shanghai is the largest, with some 12 million inhabitants; Peking, the capital, ranks second with over 9 million; Tientsin has 8 million; and Canton has more than 5 million. While these numbers may seem staggering, the fact remains that only about one-fifth of China's population lives in cities. The rest —more than 800 million people—live in the countryside. Most peasant families are crowded in modest thatched-roof farmhouses or tiny mud-brick cottages without heat or plumbing. Labor is heavy, without benefit of modern machinery, and meals are simple.

Although Han Chinese make up about 94 percent

of the population, there are about 55 other ethnic groups—Mongols, Manchus, Uygurs, and Kazakhs, to name just a few. Together they form a population of about 55 million. These peoples differ from the Han, and from each other, in culture, religion, and physical appearance. Many of them live in the remote frontier regions of the north, west, and south. The majority Han, with their long sense of cultural superiority and deep-seated distrust of outsiders, have looked down on these "national minorities" and kept them on the fringe of Chinese life. The Communist regime has designated the areas in which they live as "autonomous regions." For the sake of political stability, however, the government has begun to give them greater recognition. The national minorities are even acknowledged on the Chinese flag: against a red background, a large gold star that stands for the Han people is surrounded by four smaller stars representing the major autonomous regions.

There is another set of divisions among the Chinese people that cannot be ignored. Indeed it is the most distinct separation of all, like a series of walls that sets apart whole segments of the population. This is the division between ordinary citizens on the one hand and cadres, Party members, and military personnel on the other hand. Cadres are officials of the state, ranging from the nation's top leaders to low-level clerks and heads of village production teams. The cadres are ranked by their authority and responsibility, with corresponding wage and benefit levels. The cadres enjoy many special privileges that ordinary workers do not. Special status and prestige also are accorded to members of the Communist party. Not all cadres are party members, and not all party members are cadres. Today there are approximately 43 million members of the Communist party. Finally, soldiers and officers of the People's Liberation Army are held in great esteem. A career in the military is sought after by many of China's youth but achieved by relatively few. The training is rigorous, but the Chinese soldier is well fed and well clothed.

With all the diversities in land, climate, culture, ethnicity, and status, there are also some universal truths about life in the People's Republic today. Although the Communist system has made great strides, poverty is still widespread. There is simply too little land to feed the huge population. The overall standard of living remains low, both in the cities and the countryside. The average wage is only about 65 *yuan* ($35) per month. There are few modern conveniences, sanitation is poor, health care needs great improvement, and illiteracy is high. In many ways, China remains the "poor man of Asia."

RUMBLINGS FROM
THE SLEEPING GIANT

The China that Westerners see today is a nation undergoing rapid change. It is still a land of towering pagodas, magnificent carved jade, and exotic customs; the culture remains steeped in history and tradition. At the same time, however, the walls are beginning to come down. Doors are opening, and the outside world is being let in. Western ways are being adopted in an effort to raise the standard of living and unleash the nation's vast potential. The sleeping giant is beginning to stir.

With a new global outlook, Chinese leaders have taken an increasingly active role in world politics, exchanging visits with foreign heads of state, participating in the United Nations and other international organizations, and finding a niche for the People's Republic in the complex interrelationship of the United

Chinese villagers,
Guangdong Province

States, Soviet Union, Europe, and the Third World. In 1984, the People's Republic sent its first full-fledged team to the Olympic Games. Chinese scientists, artists, and students participate in exchange programs with other countries. And, at the center of the great shift, foreign trade and investment are growing rapidly. Chinese goods are being exported in increasing volume, and foreign-made goods—everything from Coca-Cola to Sony television sets and IBM computers—are flowing in. Foreign companies are being enlisted to help build hotels, factories, nuclear power plants, and other projects.

The changes in domestic policy have been equally dramatic. In the 1980s, the Peking regime has instituted sweeping new programs to promote Western-style capitalism. In industry and agriculture, state control is giving way to free-market competition. Individual Chinese are being allowed—indeed encouraged—to sell their own produce for profit and to set up private businesses. And along with the influx of foreign commodities and investments has come increasing acceptance of Western culture. Mao jackets are giving way to suits, dresses, and T-shirts. Peking has a fast-food restaurant. Even rock music, once labeled "bourgeois" and "decadent," is beginning to be heard.

It is a new Chinese revolution. It is not violent like the Communist revolution of the 1940s, but the new approach may prove equally far-reaching. The Chinese have a long memory and are perhaps still leery of foreign ways. Though they remain the warmest of hosts, the Chinese people—especially the elderly—will resist complete Westernization. But at the root of the new revolution is the deep, enduring pride in Chinese civilization, a desire to catch up economically and make the "Middle Kingdom" strong again. Mao Tse-tung had the goal of modernizing China and putting it in the front rank of the international community by the end of the twentieth century. Since Mao's death in 1976, however, China's new "pragmatic" leadership has recognized the limitations of his radical plan for reaching that goal.

Chapter 2
Mao's China

One of the lasting images of Mao Tse-tung's China is set during the Cultural Revolution of the late 1960s, a period of ideological fervor and severe political repression. A phalanx of Red Guards, the soldiers of Mao's grim campaign, march through Tian An Men Square in Peking. They wear bright green uniforms and caps with a prominent red star above the front rim. In their right hands they clutch small red books. As they march through the square, Chairman Mao, atop the Gate of Heavenly Peace, lifts his arm in salute. Row by row, in swift precision, the Guards raise their books and place them over their hearts.

The little red book is called *Quotations from Chairman Mao Tse-tung*. It contains the thoughts of Mao on everything from Communism and "class struggle" to women, culture, and socialist education. Compiled from speeches, interviews, and writings from as early as the 1930s. *Quotations* became the bible of the Communist Chinese state. Schoolchildren learned to recite its passages by heart—sometimes even backwards.

In a chapter entitled "Building Our Country Through Diligence and Frugality," Mao took a realistic view of China's plight:

We must see to it that all our cadres and all our people constantly bear in mind that ours is a big socialist country but an economically backward and poor one. . . . To make China rich and strong needs several decades of intense effort, which will include, among other things, the effort to practice strict economy and combat waste, i.e., the policy of building up our country through diligence and frugality.

It can be fairly concluded that Mao Tse-tung never did make China "rich and strong." During his quarter-century of rule, life in the People's Republic indeed remained frugal—at times impoverished—and diligence to his cause finally lapsed. The fact remains, however, that no leader in world history ever exerted more power over more people than Mao Tse-tung. And perhaps no leader ever put a more radical vision into practice for so long. Chairman Mao was known as "The Great Helmsman," charting his own course to prosperity and strength for China. The Communism of Mao had a distinctly Chinese imprint, as proudly independent as the ancient empire of Zhong Guo.

THE RISE OF
THE COMMUNISTS

The Chinese Communist party was formed in Shanghai in July 1921, a time of great turmoil and uncertainty. China's first constitutional president, Dr. Sun Yat-sen, and his Nationalist party (the Kuomintang) had lost control, and the country was divided among several regional warlords. World War I was over, and China was bitter over its treatment by Europe. Conflicting forces of patriotism and revolution were in the air.

In 1923, with the political and military support of

the Soviet Union, Sun Yat-sen revived the Kuomintang. The Communist party, which also had been formed with the support and advice of Moscow, joined with the Kuomintang in 1924. A joint revolutionary army was created. For the next three years, the Soviet Union, the Kuomintang, and the Communists maintained a triple alliance with the purpose of regaining control of China and restoring national sovereignty.

But then there was a break. After the death of Sun, the right wing of the Kuomintang, led by Chiang Kai-shek, gradually gained supremacy. Chiang Kai-shek ended the alliance with the Soviet Union and ousted the Communists from the Kuomintang. Anyone with leftist sympathies was executed or imprisoned, and the Communist party was forced underground. The Kuomintang, meanwhile, established the Provisional Nationalist Government, with Chiang Kai-shek as president, in April 1927. Foreign governments accorded official recognition to the Nanking-based regime in 1928.

Over the next decade, Chiang Kai-shek sought to unify China under the Nationalist government and to annihilate the Communists. He succeeded at neither. Warlords retained control of several provinces, Japan took over much of the north and east, and the Communists remained very much alive.

The seeds of success for the Communist revolution lay in the countryside. When the Kuomintang suppressed the Communists in the cities, they moved their base to Jiangxi Province in the southeast. When Chiang Kai-shek's army expelled them from Jiangxi Province in 1934, the Communists began their famous Long March—6,000 miles (9,600 km) northwest to Shaanxi Province. It was during the Long March that Mao Tse-tung emerged as the undisputed leader of the Chinese Communists. Mao had long believed that a proletarian, or labor class, revolution in China would have to rely on the peasant population. The Russian advisers who had worked with the early Chinese Communists in the 1920s believed that the revolution should follow the Soviet pattern and begin in the cities. But Mao realized that China's peasantry had suffered great hardship and would be ripe for change. Moreover, the ideal military strategy would be guerrilla warfare based in the countryside. The Russians actually tried to stop Mao's peasant-based movement, but the "Great Helmsman" had charted the right course. Support for the Communists grew rapidly among the peasant population.

During the World War II years, Mao and the Communists solidified their base in the Chinese countryside. By 1945 they governed millions of peasants in several northern regions. Their program of reform and their armed resistance to the Japanese invaders won a wide following, and by the end of the war the party had one million actual members. By contrast, the Nationalist government of Chiang Kai-shek had been severely weakened by internal dissension and corruption. When World War II was over, the United States tried to bring the Communists and Nationalists together. The effort failed, and full-scale civil war broke out in 1947. Employing brilliant guerrilla warfare tactics and offering a more attractive reform program to the Chinese people, Mao and the Communists emerged victorious. After a series of catastrophic military defeats, Chiang Kai-shek and the remnants of his Nationalist government fled to Taiwan in 1949.

THE PEOPLE'S REPUBLIC

On October 1, 1949, Mao Tse-tung proclaimed the People's Republic of China. "The Chinese people have stood up," he declared. "Our state is a people's democratic dictatorship, led by the working class and based on the worker-peasant alliance. The aim of this dictatorship is to protect all our people so that they can devote themselves to peaceful labor and build China into a socialist country with a modern industry, agriculture, science and culture."

There was much to do. China had suffered decades of division and warfare. The means of production were severely crippled. Local and provincial government had broken down. Industry was in shambles. The Communists realized, therefore, that their first task was to consolidate power and start rebuilding—to sweep away old systems and establish new institutions of government.

The system they devised included three major organizations: the Chinese Communist party (CCP), the state apparatus, and the People's Liberation Army (PLA). Most of the power was centered in the CCP. Today, as then, the party determines national policies and controls the army; the state apparatus carries out the party's policy directives.

The most important group within the CCP is the Central Committee. The chairman of the Central Committee is normally the paramount leader of the People's Republic; Mao Tse-tung was the first chairman of the Central Committee. Within the Central Committee, the real power rests with the twenty-seven-member Political Bureau (Politburo) and the seven-member Standing Committee; the Politburo and Standing Committee meet regularly to set basic policies. Finally, the Central Committee includes the Military Affairs Commission, through which the party controls the armed forces. The Military Commission has its own chairman, but it is usually dominated by the top leadership of the Central Committee.

The state apparatus also is composed of several

Mao Tse-tung (right) and Chou En-lai.
Mao and Chou took part in
the revolution and, after 1949,
Chou became China's foreign
minister and later, premier.
After Mao, he was the second
most powerful man in China.

bodies. The highest of these is the National People's Congress (NPC), made up of several thousand deputies elected to five-year terms by provincial people's congresses. The real authority in the state apparatus, however, lies in the State Council, the executive organ of the NPC. It is made up of the premier, two vice premiers, and the ministers in charge of some forty ministries and commissions. These ministries and commissions are charged with carrying out specific party policies in such areas as agriculture, defense, and finance.

Finally, since its founding in 1927 (as the Red Army) the PLA has been a major political force in China. Military campaigns were of course central to the Communists' rise to power, and the army continues to play a wider role than just national defense. The top military officers carry considerable clout within the regime.

Having declared the People's Republic and established the three institutions of power, Mao Tse-tung embarked on the enormous tasks of consolidation and reconstruction. Emphasis was placed on recruiting young people and creating enthusiasm for Marxist-Leninist ideology. At the same time, "enemies of the people"—businessmen, intellectuals, and professionals—were eliminated. And perhaps most significantly, Mao's land-reform program was expanded to the national level. Property owners and landlords were stripped of their possessions, and the land was distributed equally among the peasantry.

"THE BAMBOO CURTAIN"

Among the first acts of the new Chinese regime was to cut all ties with the West. Great Britain and the

United States were regarded as the chief enemies. The British were considered villains because of their trade practices, the Opium War, and the Boxer Rebellion. China's new leaders quickly instituted severe restrictions against British merchants, and within a few short years all British businessmen had left the mainland. The United States, meanwhile, was considered the most dangerous foreign enemy. Washington opposed the Communist regime from the beginning, recognizing the Nationalists on Taiwan as the legitimate government of China. The hostility intensified in 1950, when China entered the Korean War in support of North Korea and against U.S.-supported South Korea. At that time also, the United States began sending military aid to the hated Chiang Kai-shek on Taiwan.

Although several Western European countries (including Great Britain) extended formal recognition to the People's Republic in 1949 and 1950, Mao had fundamental ideological differences that did not allow him to reciprocate. The nations of the West were "bourgeois capitalists" and "imperialist running dogs." And so, just as the Soviet Union had set up the Iron Curtain around Eastern Europe, China now cloaked itself behind a "bamboo curtain." For decades the West knew little of what went on inside.

During the early years of Communist rule, Peking did maintain close relations with its geographic and ideological neighbor, the Soviet Union. Moscow had aligned itself with the fledgling CCP in the 1920s, and the Chinese Communists now looked to the USSR as a sort of model for their own system. The Chinese followed the basic military structure used by the Soviets, as well as the organization of the police, strategies of economic development, and, of course, the basic principles of Marxism-Leninism. The Soviets provided considerable military and economic aid,

Mao and Premier Nikita Khrushchev
of the Soviet Union before
the Sino-Soviet split

everything from weapons and advisers to engineering plans for factories and dams.

In the winter of 1949–50, Mao made his first visit abroad as the leader of the People's Republic, spending ten weeks in the Soviet Union. The result of his long negotiations with Soviet leader Joseph Stalin was a thirty-year treaty of friendship and alliance. The pact included a $300 million loan to the Peking government.

China's "friendship and alliance" with the Soviet Union did not last the thirty years. For a variety of complex reasons, relations between the two Communist giants began to deteriorate in the late 1950s. The differences were ideological, territorial, and strategic. The ideological differences went back to the 1930s, when Mao resisted the Soviet prescription for an urban-based Communist revolution (as envisioned by Marx). The real rift began to develop after the death of Stalin in 1953, with the rise of Nikita Khrushchev as the top Soviet leader. In 1956 the new Kremlin chief began to denounce the excesses of Stalin's rule, and in 1957 he met with U.S. President Dwight Eisenhower. Mao was enraged. He felt the Soviets under Khrushchev were slipping into "revisionism" and "consumer communism." Moreover, China was beginning to get restless with its status as the Soviets' "younger brother."

Subsequent events hastened the Sino-Soviet split. In 1958, as a gesture of its desire to "liberate" Taiwan, China began intensive shelling of the Nationalist-held island of Quemoy. Moscow refused to support the bombing and opposed any plans for a Chinese takeover of Taiwan. Then in 1959, China attacked Indian forces on the Kashmir frontier, and the Soviets offered arms to India. By 1960 the break between China and the USSR had come fully into the open. Moscow recalled its technical advisers, demanded repayment of all its loans, and halted economic aid.

Very much at the core of the Sino-Soviet dispute was China's longstanding fear of foreign intrusion. China and the Soviet Union share the world's longest border, several thousand miles of indefensible terrain. Disputes over the frontier go back many centuries. The Chinese believe that Russians stole huge amounts of territory in the seventeenth, eighteenth, and nineteenth centuries. Perhaps with justification, Peking now was suspicious that the Soviets were building a military force along the border and were planning an invasion. Nothing could have struck a more tender nerve. By 1969 there were serious border clashes between China and the USSR along the Ussuri River. The fighting eventually subsided, but the People's Republic and the Soviet Union had become bitter rivals.

Thus, during his first decade in power, Mao Tsetung—the "Great Helmsman"—had steered China on a radically independent course. The People's Republic was all but alone in international waters, maintaining few ties with the world community. The remnants of Western imperialism had been expelled. Fear and disdain had led to a break with the Soviet Union. Modest ties were established with the Third World, but China had basically shut itself in. The "bamboo curtain," like another Great Wall, had been raised to keep out barbarians. What went on behind it remained very much a mystery to the world at large, and China again came to be viewed as a "sleeping giant."

THE HUNDRED FLOWERS, GREAT LEAP, AND CULTURAL REVOLUTION

Inside the People's Republic, Mao went about building a society based on Marxist-Leninist principles. While a major economic and social revolution in its own right, the land-reform program had been only a start. During the early 1950s, Peking's new Communist leadership began a process of full collectivization. Unlike the Soviet Union, which moved almost directly into a system of collective farming, China progressed in stages. The next step after basic land reform was a system based on "mutual aid teams"—fifteen to thirty families together working a plot of land. The land was still privately owned, but a Communist cadre was on hand to supervise its use. Then came a phase of "agricultural producers cooperatives," in which three or four mutual aid teams pooled their land, labor, animals, tools, and produce; now the land was managed according to state plans. Finally, the cooperatives were transformed into collective farms; the state took full ownership and paid the farmers for their labor.

The entire economic and social order of China was being reshaped. Local decision-making gave way to centralized authority. Political power and economic planning lay exclusively in Peking. Private ownership had been virtually abolished. Everything belonged to, and was produced for, the People. Even art, literature, and education were to be committed to the Communist ideal. The party and state asserted strict control over intellectual and cultural affairs.

By 1957, Mao believed that the majority of Chinese, including academics and intellectuals, had been won over to his radical socialist thinking. That spring, therefore, he issued a speech encouraging greater freedom of expression and inviting criticism of his regime. "Let a hundred flowers bloom, let a hundred schools of thought contend," he said. The relaxation of political controls and the opening up to criticism became known as the Hundred Flowers Campaign; it wilted quickly. The criticisms were louder and more severe than Mao had anticipated, and he reacted sharply. Critics were forced to declare their errors, and many intellectuals were punished.

With the failure of the Hundred Flowers Campaign, Mao was increasingly concerned about the commitment of the Chinese people to his new ethic. And so he proceeded to institute even more radical policies, to step up propaganda, and to repress all forms of criticism and free thought. This shift to the left culminated in an economic program called the "Great Leap Forward," which lasted from 1958 to 1960. Among other things, the Great Leap Forward took the process of collectivization one step further, as cooperative farms were consolidated into larger "people's communes." In these communes, which were created in cities as well as the countryside, member families shared common kitchens and mess halls; work assignments were rotated; and care of children and the aged was collective.

The Great Leap Forward also targeted enormous increases in both agricultural and industrial production. Economic planners believed that China could become a modern industrial power if the peasantry worked hard and ran small rural factories. Steel, for example, would be manufactured in "backyard furnaces." But again Peking's plans failed. Lack of coordination, neglect of crops, two years of bad weather, and the withdrawal of Soviet advisers resulted in severe shortages of food and widespread famine.

Mao Tse-tung suffered a loss of power and prestige as a result of the failed Great Leap Forward. Cracks began to appear in party unity, as certain high officials expressed disagreement with the direction of policy. Mao retrenched and let the tide recede, but he still had much to prove. His first order of business would be to oust all adversaries and reaffirm his power and prestige. Beyond that he aimed to purify the party and the entire country of bourgeois culture, decadent thinking, and imperialist corruption. He yearned to succeed at his own brand of Communism without help from the Soviets. He still sought to vindicate his faith in the peasantry. And he intended to vent his hatred of intellectuals.

The result was the Great Proletarian Cultural Revolution, launched in 1966. The next three years were marked by extreme repression, widespread purges, and a wave of state terrorism. Students and young workers faithful to Mao were organized into the powerful Red Guard, which carried out his mission. Books, records, paintings, and any other materials not in the revolutionary spirit were confiscated. Prerevolutionary customs and traditions were forbidden. Mao's enemies within the Party were eliminated. Teachers, intellectuals, and bureaucrats with "bad class background" were harassed, tortured, or killed. Other undesirables were removed to the countryside to perform menial labor. Millions of urban teenagers were separated from their families and sent to work on agricultural communes. "This is one class overthrowing another," said Mao simply.

Calm was restored in 1969, but Mao's Cultural Revolution had been an economic, social, and political disaster, as well as a horrible nightmare for millions of Chinese. By the government's own estimate, 100 million young people ended up illiterate. The economy was set back decades, as qualified engineers and technicians were shipped off to the countryside, untrained workers became factory managers, and the industrial plant fell into disrepair. Valuable years of education were lost, health care was neglected, art and literature were stifled, and families were broken up. Finally, the Chinese people—Mao's great "worker-peasant" alliance—were deeply disillusioned. Their

revolutionary zeal was gone. The feeling could not openly be expressed, but enthusiasm for the Maoist ideal clearly had waned.

PING-PONG, RECONCILIATION, AND THE DEATH OF MAO

During the convulsive years of the Cultural Revolution, China's influence in the world fell to its lowest level. The door was still shut tight against the West, relations with the Soviet Union continued to deteriorate, and several smaller Communist countries had drifted into the Soviet sphere. Peking finally seemed to grow concerned when the U.S. and USSR opened the Strategic Arms Limitation Talks (SALT) in 1969. Fearing that Washington and Moscow might strengthen ties and leave the Chinese in the cold, Peking apparently began to consider some measure of reconciliation with the United States. The clearest signal was its reluctance to intervene directly in the Vietnam War.

The United States made its own cautious moves toward reconciliation. During the first two years of the Nixon administration, the United States eased restrictions on trade with the People's Republic and loosened restrictions on American travel to the Chinese mainland.

The ice was finally broken, oddly enough, at a ping-pong tournament in April 1971. At the world table

Red Guards staging a skit on the theme of "Down with U.S. Imperialism," 1967

In 1972, President Nixon met with
China's leader, Mao Tse-tung.

tennis tournament in Japan, the Chinese government invited the U.S. team to visit the People's Republic. The invitation, said the Chinese, was "for the sake of promoting friendship between the peoples of China and the United States."

The next few months saw several more diplomatic breakthroughs. In July 1971, President Nixon accepted an invitation to visit China. In October 1971, the United Nations voted to seat the People's Republic of China and to oust the Nationalist Republic of China (Taiwan). And in February 1972, President Nixon made his historic journey. At the conclusion of his trip, the U.S. and Chinese governments issued the Shanghai Communiqué, declaring a mutual desire for "normalization of relations."

A ping-pong team and President Nixon (along with diplomats and journalists) thus became the first Americans allowed inside China since the Communist revolution. There had been noticeable changes. The Communists had done a great deal to reduce poverty and hunger; grain production and life expectancy both had *doubled* since 1949. Nevertheless, conditions were still grim. Food staples were carefully rationed. Cities were overcrowded, and factories and equipment were badly out of date. In the countryside, plows were still being pulled by oxen. The Cultural Revolution had left deep wounds, and the people were disillusioned. Life everywhere was gray and austere.

Mao Tse-tung was 78 years old when he welcomed President Nixon to the People's Republic of China. He had spent nearly a quarter-century struggling to establish a Communist state and another quarter-century struggling to keep the revolution moving forward. Now he was tiring, and his health was beginning to fail. Though Mao was ill for the last years of his life and the maneuvering for power was already under way, basic changes in the course of Chinese socialism would await his death—on September 9, 1976.

Chapter 3

The Quiet Revolution

In April 1984, the government-run *Peking Daily* published a photo of chicken farmer Sun Guiying standing proudly with her family beside a brand new Toyota automobile: Sun had just become the first Chinese peasant to buy a private car since the Communists came to power. In the city of Chengdu, Sichuan Province, the ambitious Wu Shiyuan borrowed a few hundred *yuan* and opened the Delicious Taste Self-Managed Restaurant. Today in Shanghai and elsewhere, the streets are lined with colorful signs picturing television sets, videocassette recorders, and cameras. A new company outside Canton sells common stock. And in Shenzhen, once a modest fishing village, the lavish Honey Lake Country Club features a sprawling golf course. A nearby billboard carries an imposing message: "Time is Money! Efficiency is Life!"

During the spring of 1984, U.S. President Ronald Reagan went on a five-day "journey for peace" to the People's Republic of China. He did not ride in Sun Guiying's Toyota or play on the Honey Lake golf course, but the China he did see was very different from the Spartan society witnessed by President Nixon in 1972. All was not country clubs and modern appliances—

far from it—but there had been startling changes. More than 10 million Chinese were now working in small private businesses and do-it-yourself trades— eighty times more than in 1978. Communes were being dismantled, and farmers were selling their surplus crops for profit. Consumer purchasing was being encouraged by the state. In politics, economy, lifestyle, and culture, a new revolution was under way in the People's Republic. It was a quiet, nonviolent revolution, but the transformations it brought were potentially as far-reaching and dramatic as those of the Communist changeover of the 1950s.

What had happened to Mao Tse-tung's "dictatorship of the proletariat"? Had the "just struggle against capitalism" been abandoned? Where had the "glorious road of socialism" finally led?

HUA, DENG, AND
THE GANG OF FOUR

On the Chinese calendar, 1976 was the Year of the Dragon. In Peking and throughout the People's Republic, the dragon breathed fire. Death and purge in the highest ranks of government kindled a fierce struggle for political power, ideological supremacy, and the direction of the socialist revolution. The convulsions in Peking were surpassed only by a violent earthquake in the nearby city of Tangshan that killed 650,000 people. According to Chinese legend, natural disasters signal the end of one ruling dynasty and the beginning of another.

The first shock came in January, when Premier Chou En-lai, Mao's second-in-command and heir apparent, died in Peking. Mao, too, had been ailing for some time, and the passing of Chou set off a fight for power between radical Maoists and moderate reformers (of which Chou had been one). The premiership ended up with an apparent compromise figure, the relatively unknown Hua Guofeng.

Key players in the drama that had been unfolding were Deng Xiaoping, a moderate senior vice-premier, and a small group of radical leftists led by Jiang Qing, the wife of Mao. Jiang, a former actress, had become one of Peking's most powerful figures during the Cultural Revolution. Deng, who had been with Mao since the Long March of the 1930s, had used his power to promote liberal economic reforms. In the fury of the Cultural Revolution, Jiang and the radicals labeled Deng a "capitalist roader," stripped him of his power, and paraded him through Peking wearing a dunce cap. By 1973, after relative calm had been restored, Deng was "rehabilitated" and began reconsolidating his power. Jiang and the radicals, nevertheless, continued to wield an iron hand. They remained staunch enemies of reform and managed to have several members of the Politburo purged, including Deng again in April 1976.

Hua Guofeng, meanwhile, was in an uncertain position. Though Mao was ill, his presence still set a limit on Hua's authority. Moreover, as long as Mao was alive, Jiang Qing held formidable power. That situation changed dramatically with Mao's death on September 9. Within one month, Jiang and three other radical leaders were thrown in prison for attempting a coup. They were labeled the "Gang of Four" and blamed for virtually every problem China had suffered since the mid-1960s. At the same time, Hua released thousands of political prisoners that had been held since the Cultural Revolution. He also restored scores of party and state moderates who had been purged over the years. Among them was Deng Xiaoping, who thus proved to be the most resilient figure in modern Chinese politics. By the summer of 1977, Deng had been returned to the Politburo and his old posts of senior vice-premier, vice-chairman of the party, and vice-chairman of the Military Commission. Hua himself headed the state, party, and Military Commission.

Hua and Deng sought to reestablish the moderate economic policies of reform and modernization that had been extinguished by the Maoist radicals. Along with this loosening of economic restraints came a limited relaxation of political control and a removal of some bans on personal and artistic expression. For a time, the regime even tolerated underground magazines and the posting of protest literature on Peking's "Democracy Wall." Also notable at this time was the process of "de-Maoification," in which the new leaderships sought to quell any reverence for Mao's teachings. And in January 1981, the Gang of Four and six other defendants were found guilty of counterrevolutionary activities. Their convictions ranged from sixteen years in prison to a suspended death sentence for Jiang Qing. Thus, less than five years after his death, Mao was being de-sanctified, his wife was behind bars, and his Communist ideal was being unraveled.

Indeed, other changes had already taken place in China's top leadership. Behind the moderates he had led in the 1960s and restored in 1977–78, Deng gradually wrested control from Hua Guofeng. In 1980 he forced Hua to resign and replaced him with his own men: Zhao Ziyang became premier, and Hu Yaobang became chairman of the Communist party. Deng, the dominant power and final decision-maker, had himself named chairman of the Military Commission. Deng Xiaoping—who had spent five years in France as a youth, who had been vilified as a "capitalist roader" during the Cultural Revolution, and who even professed a love for gourmet food—now was at the helm of the Communist revolution. And the course he

*Deng Xiaoping (center) inspecting
an electronics company*

charted was very different from the one drawn by the "Great Helmsman."

CATCHING MICE

Underlying the policy changes of Deng Xiaoping was a fundamental shift in ideology—the introduction of new goals and precepts for the Communist revolution. The post-Mao leadership still supported the four revolutionary principles—pursuit of socialism, dictatorship of the proletariat, supremacy of the Chinese Communist party, and Marxism-Leninism-Mao Thought —but the principles were being interpreted in fundamentally different ways. The radical egalitarianism and "class struggle" championed by Mao were dismissed, and the clarions were being sounded for pragmatism, productivity, and progress.

The denunciations of Maoist "leftist errors" have at times been harsh. In February 1985, party leader Hu Yaobang declared that the Mao Communists had "wasted twenty years with radical leftist nonsense." In April 1984, the *People's Daily* (the official English-language government newspaper) decried the "poisonous legacy" of the radical left. Another official publication attacked the principle of Maoist egalitarianism: "experience proves that egalitarianism is a disaster to the socialist cause, a throttle on enthusiasm for labor, and a corrosive agent to social productive forces."

"Productive forces" is one of the key phrases in the new way of thinking and the new propaganda. The dismantling of communes and the institution of capitalist principles have been presented as simple, practical measures to increase productivity and improve the quality of life. They represent refinements of the socialist system, not abandonments of it. They free the system from dogma and unleash the "productive forces" of the Chinese masses.

The regime has gone so far as to urge Chinese workers to pursue wealth. Getting rich and buying a car, they are told, is not decadent if life is made more pleasant. More importantly, according to Deng, "to make some people rich first leads all the people to wealth." What remains decadent and bourgeois is pleasure-seeking without work, reward without productivity. To help make that point, the State Council in 1985 declared a new policy for all government offices: *xiuxi*, the traditional after-lunch siesta, would be banned.

Few would regard the banning of afternoon naps as an ideological revolution, but the step did typify Deng's new approach; it was a simple, practical measure to get China working. Indeed, Deng's ideology was in many ways a rejection of ideology itself. Practice, not theory, became "the sole criterion of truth." Action, not dogma, would unleash China's "productive forces." Individual initiative and hard work, not doctrines and slogans, would make China great again. The emphasis on practical results and the rejection of ideology—Maoist or otherwise—were summed up by Deng Xiaoping in an often-quoted saying: "It doesn't matter whether a cat is black or white, as long as it catches mice."

The Chinese people have welcomed Deng's pragmatism with open arms. Embittered, exhausted, and alienated by the Cultural Revolution, many Chinese are simply fed up with ideology. Despite the real improvements brought by Mao's Communism, farmers and factory workers had suffered many shortages and privations. The popular attitude was summed up by a government official: "Most people today don't care whether something is capitalist or socialist. They just want their lives to improve."

While rejecting a dogmatic approach, Deng's economic planners have established formal goals and overall strategies. There are, after all, mice to catch. In setting their objectives and designing a development plan, the new leaders have sought to avoid the mistakes of Mao. They see at least two major errors in Mao's economic policies. First, he had set production targets too high and speeded development too fast. Expecting too much too soon had led to such failures as the Great Leap Forward. Second, Mao had overemphasized heavy industry at the expense of light industry and consumer goods. Deng and his pragmatic colleagues certainly have their own high ambitions: to quadruple the gross national product and raise the average annual income from less than $150 in 1980 to $800 by the year 2000. The overall emphasis, however, will be on slow transformation: institute market reforms and modernize facilities in the 1980s to allow more rapid growth in the 1990s. As for special emphasis, priority will be given to light industry. As Chinese workers gain greater purchasing power, they will be able to buy more appliances and other consumer goods. The government will subsidize these industries until they can stand alone.

All in all, Deng's pragmatic approach has resulted in a "mixed economy," a combination of limited free-market capitalism and socialist state ownership. The economic program has been dubbed the "Four Modernizations," for the general sectors targeted for development. In order of priority, the four sectors are: agriculture, industry, science and technology, and defense.

AGRICULTURE □ The first and most far-reaching changes have come in the agricultural sector. Some 80 percent of the Chinese population—more than 800 million people—live in the countryside. The agricultural reforms, therefore, affect the largest number of Chinese. Land has not been returned to private ownership; it is still owned by the state. Under the new system, however, the Chinese peasant has more direct control over how it is used. The whole process of collectivization instituted under Mao—from mutual aid teams to cooperatives, to collectives, to communes —is being dismantled. In its place, the Deng regime has established a system in which the individual farmer is not paid for how many hours he works but for how much he produces. There are rewards and incentives for greater output. "Efficiency Is Life!"

The centerpiece of Deng's agricultural reform program is the "household responsibility" system. Under this system, the individual peasant family is assigned part of a field and makes a production contract with local officials of the state. The contract establishes a particular use of the land, growing cotton or raising poultry, for example, and sets the amount and price of goods to be sold to the state. After this state quota has been filled, the farmer is free to sell surplus produce for profit. The state itself will buy it at a markup of 50 percent, or the farmer can sell it at open market for whatever price he can get. In the countryside and cities alike, bustling "free markets" have opened for peasants to sell their goods.

When the system of "household responsibility" was first instituted in 1979, many peasants hesitated to make contract commitments because they were afraid the government would change its mind—as it had so many times before. To reassure them, the state extended the length of contracts from one to three years to fifteen years. The government has also added other incentives and refinements. To boost grain production, for example, it has increased the price it will pay for surplus by 23 percent.

By propaganda as well as by economic incentive,

Early morning shoppers line up to buy
fresh beans on a Shanghai street corner.
Farm workers from a nearby collective
sell the surplus from their
production contract with the state.

the Peking leadership has encouraged farmers to supplement their incomes by raising pigs, planting orchards, or growing vegetables as sideline businesses. That, it feels, will lead to overall expansion and growth. Said Party leader Hu Yaobang: "After the peasants become rich, we must guide them to invest ... in development projects." The strategy is reminiscent of that of the Great Leap Forward, in which Mao looked to the countryside for major development projects and economic diversification. The differences, however, are fundamental. The new agricultural reforms do not take peasants away from their plots to build "backyard furnaces"; they encourage *greater* farm production. Also, they do not establish unreasonable production quotas without rewarding the worker. And most importantly, they do not dogmatically oppose capitalist, free-market incentives; rather, they spur production precisely by giving the peasant greater individual responsibility.

INDUSTRY □ In October 1984, a full five years after the introduction of agricultural reform, the Communist Party Central Committee announced plans for similarly sweeping changes in the industrial economy. The lapse in time reflected Peking's gradual approach to economic growth, avoiding the abrupt policy shifts and unrealistic expectations of Mao. The new industrial measures, however, would ultimately do for China's 200 million urban dwellers what the agricultural reforms did for its 800 million rural population. Together, the industrial and agricultural reforms would complete the boldest economic experiment ever attempted by a major Communist power.

In its document announcing the industrial reforms, the Central Committee called for the abandonment of "excessive and rigid control over enterprises" by state ministries. Under the old Stalinist system, the government maintained all planning and decision-making authority over China's one million state-owned enterprises. Now much of that authority would be turned over directly to plant managers. Factories and other enterprises still would be owned by the state—preserving socialism—but on-site managers would become responsible for planning, marketing, use of capital, and distribution of profits. "In short," the document stated, "the enterprise would truly be made a relatively independent economic entity."

As an "independent economic entity," each enterprise would be responsible for its own survival. It would compete against other enterprises, and its success or failure would be determined by principles of supply and demand. "Our enterprises are put to the test of direct judgment by consumers in the marketplace so that only the best survive," said the Central Committee.

The key to the entire reform, the document stated, was a fundamental change in the way prices are fixed. Under the old system, the government set the prices for all commodities; it used the price structure to spur some industries and slow others down. This, it was now realized, had led to "endless wrangling and much confusion." Under the new system, price determination (within a specified range) would be left to plant managers. Commodities would be priced so as to reflect their market value and the relation of supply to demand. Plant managers would set prices as part of their competitive strategies.

Another important area of capitalist-style reform has been pay incentive, hiring, firing, and promotion. Previously, workers had received a standard flat wage of 30 to 35 yuan per month, no matter how much or how little they produced. Children inherited factory jobs from retiring parents. Criminal offense was about the only cause for firing a worker. And promotion was based on seniority and political "purity." It amounted to a system of guaranteed employment, known as the "iron rice bowl." Now, having to compete for survival, enterprises are abandoning the "iron rice bowl" in favor of a system based on productivity. Wages are determined by an employee's skill and efficiency, with bonuses if business is good. Jobs are awarded on the basis of training and competence, rarely through inheritance. Promotions are based on efficiency and output. And firings are becoming commonplace. The old Marxist doctrine of "to each according to his need" has given way to a principle more reminiscent of Adam Smith: "more pay for more work and less pay for less work."

SCIENCE AND TECHNOLOGY □ The third of the Four Modernizations has been a campaign to advance Chinese science and technology. The radical socialism of Mao Tse-tung had stifled basic research and development by persecuting intellectuals, isolating China from outside contacts, and leaving innovation to the overworked, undereducated, politically conscious masses. Recognizing that there is much catching up to do, the new Peking leadership has taken an aggressive, two-pronged approach to scientific and technological modernization.

For the immediate purpose of streamlining industry, modernizing agriculture, upgrading medical care, and setting up its own high-tech production facilities, China has looked to the outside for help. Through trade agreements, exchange programs, and joint ventures, the United States, Japan, and Western Europe have helped install a broad variety of new technologies and helped train the Chinese in operation, maintenance, and production.

For the long term, the Peking leadership has taken steps to ensure China's own capabilities in basic

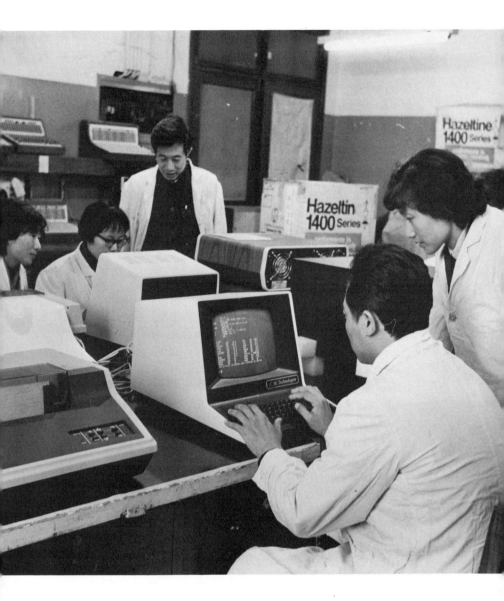

Researchers operating a U.S.-made computer.
China is importing machinery and
electronic products from the United States
to improve its technology.

research and development. The introduction of competitive forces in the industrial sector itself promotes technological innovation: the more efficient the plant, the greater its chances of market success. In addition, institutes of scientific research are receiving healthy subsidies from the government. Intellectuals and technicians are being returned from the countryside, where they had been banished during the Cultural Revolution. Tens of thousands of Chinese students are being sent abroad for advanced technical training. And educational institutions from the primary to the post-secondary levels are putting heavy emphasis on mathematics, science, and engineering.

DEFENSE □ Of the Four Modernizations, defense has probably received the lowest priority. The People's Liberation Army is the world's largest armed force (4.2 million strong), and China has had a nuclear capability since the mid-1960s. According to military analysts, however, the Chinese military is outdated in many areas. Mao's military planning had been based on a strategy of People's War, "drowning the invaders in a sea of humanity." Although nuclear weapons and delivery systems continued to be developed, progress lagged far behind that of the United States and Soviet Union. More importantly, conventional weapons and equipment fell badly out of date. China's guns, vehicles, and other materiel are perhaps twenty years behind those of the superpowers. The new Peking leadership has avoided large arms purchases and military aid from abroad, refusing to align itself so strongly with either Washington or Moscow. To preserve its strategic and diplomatic independence, Peking has opted to rearm with its own resources. But because the main emphasis has been on economic reform and technological modernization, that process has been relatively slow.

In the spirit of efficiency and pragmatism, however, reform of the military has kept pace with the changes throughout Chinese society. In 1965, following the principle of Maoist egalitarianism, military ranks had been abolished in the PLA. In August 1984, in the new spirit of incentive and competition, badges of rank were restored. Advancement would be based on merit rather than on seniority or ideological purity.

"TAILS OF CAPITALISM"

Deng Xiaoping's "quiet" economic revolution has gone beyond the "household responsibility" system, beyond increased independence for industrial enterprises, and beyond the loosening of state authority. Indeed it has gone so far as to promote privately owned businesses and to give up state-owned enterprises to private management. In agriculture, the government has allowed the expansion of some private plots for out-and-out free-enterprise farming. On that land, peasants are free to choose their own crops, target their own markets, buy their own tractors, and even (within limits) hire their own workers. In industry and commerce, the government has invited private entrepreneurs to set up businesses that compete with state enterprises. On a smaller scale, Peking has been issuing millions of licenses for shops, free-market booths, and other modest entrepreneurships. And finally, in addition to encouraging business start-ups, the government has been turning over unsuccessful state-owned enterprises to private individuals or collectives. Once branded "tails of capitalism" to be chopped off, private businesses have now grown back in a big way. From farms and factories to curbside restaurants, bicycle repair shops, and free-market clothing stalls, capitalist enterprises have attracted increasing numbers of Chinese. By 1984, more than 6 million people owned or worked in private businesses.

MAKING CHINA
GREAT AGAIN?

Echoing a long-held Chinese aspiration, Deng Xiaoping declared that the purpose of his new brand of socialism was "to make the country rich and strong again." By the end of 1984, six years into the "quiet" revolution, it had become clear that Deng's aggressive reform policies had represented a possible first step in the direction of prosperity and strength. The ambitious goals of the Four Modernization program were appearing more and more realistic. Output targets for dozens of agricultural and industrial products were being met years ahead of schedule. The grain harvest in 1984 reached a record 400 million tons, enough to make China self-sufficient in staple food for the first time in its history, according to Peking. The value of industrial production rose by more than 10 percent in 1983 and 1984. And, thanks in large part to the responsibility system and free enterprise, the average annual income for peasants more than doubled between 1978 and 1984; urban incomes were expected to follow suit once the industrial reforms fully took hold.

The improvements, of course, go beyond statistics. While the overall standard of living remains low compared with that of the West, a growing prosperity is clearly evident throughout the People's Republic. Higher incomes and the government's new emphasis on consumer goods have enabled ordinary workers to buy many items that could not be afforded (or that were not available at all) only a few years ago. The traditional "three rounds" for which ordinary Chinese once saved—a bicycle, a wristwatch, and a sewing

Window shoppers on a fashionable Peking shopping street admire the latest in men's fashions. The blue and olive Mao jackets so prevalent for decades are slowly giving way to Western style clothes.

machine—has given way to the "three new pieces"—
a washing machine, a refrigerator, and an electric fan.
There is even a budding real-estate market, as thousands of private individuals, a new wealthy class, are
beginning to buy their own apartments.

With such enticing material incentives and with
the freedom to strike out on their own, the Chinese
people are now pursuing their own personal wealth
and well-being with as much energy and enthusiasm
as they once demonstrated for Mao's socialist revolution. They have long yearned for a chance at a better
life, and they are finding resourceful new ways to
achieve it. As more and more Chinese have more and
more money to spend, the opportunities for profitable
ventures expand even further. Private inns are being
established for those wealthy enough to take vaca-
tions. In Peking, an agency for hiring cooks, nurse-
maids, and other household help has opened for
business. The government, of course, encourages
such resourceful entrepreneurship under the theory
that prosperity breeds more prosperity.

The "quiet" revolution is not problem-free. In agriculture, for example, the furious pursuit of profits has
led to overcultivation and rapid erosion of the land in
many regions. In industry, machine maintenance has
been similarly neglected. Moreover, the development
of essential support industries, such as transportation
and energy, has not kept pace with manufacturing
growth. And there are other problems. Workers are
staying away from their regular jobs to pursue their
sideline ventures. Unlicensed enterprises are doing a
substantial business without paying taxes. Regulatory
controls are insufficient to prevent price gouging and
other unfair practices. The government is still spending up to 40 percent of its budget on subsidies, giving
certain types of businesses, and even individual
enterprises, favored status.

Despite the zeal with which the Chinese are taking advantage of the economic reforms, there is an underlying doubt as to how long the new freedom will last. Many Chinese admit to being baffled by all the abrupt changes in party policy over a mere four decades. With all the plans, programs, campaigns, and systems they have seen—each one promoted by heady propaganda—the people are uncertain about what to trust and what to expect for the future.

Just how far the "quiet" revolution will go remains open to speculation. What does seem clear, however, is that Peking is deeply committed to the new approach. Deng Xiaoping, who survived two purges under the Mao regime, has never wavered from his pragmatic approach. Having lived to see it implemented, he has taken every step to ensure that it will survive. Die-hard Maoists in the political and military power structures have been removed, and the administrative bodies of government have been revamped to fit the new system. That alone would make it hard to go back. Moreover, unlike the Great Leap Forward and other Maoist experiments, the Four Modernizations is being welcomed by the people and actually seems to be working. And, as perhaps the greatest commitment of all, the Deng regime has ended China's long isolation and opened up to outside influences. In addition to trade, joint business ventures, and other economic contacts with the world at large, the Chinese people are being exposed to new ways of thinking that cannot be erased.

Chapter 4
Opening Up

Busloads of tourists, armed with cameras and guide-books, arrive at the Great Wall outside Peking. After hiking its ramparts and taking in the view, they browse the souvenir shops and cool off at the refreshment stands back at the bottom. They buy Great Wall T-shirts and sip Coca-Cola. They relax to the piped-in music of Kenny Rogers, Otis Redding, and the Beatles. Then they board their buses and return to the shimmering, twenty-two-story Great Wall Hotel on the fringe of Peking. That night they can sample the hotel's ten restaurants and lounges, then dance under the flashing lights of a disco. Those in the group who venture outside the hotel can eat in a downtown fast-food restaurant or else pay seventy dollars a head at the plush Maxim's de Pékin.

Meanwhile, in the streets of Peking and other cities, young men wearing jeans or formal suits walk arm-in-arm with young women wearing jeans or

Teenagers dancing at a disco in Peking. The cover charge is 10 yuan or about $4.

dresses that rise boldly to the knee. They might be going to a state-sponsored dance or a rock 'n' roll concert by a group called the Mainland Band. Or else they might be spending a quiet evening watching television—*60 Minutes*, the Rose Bowl, a Dr. Seuss special, or some other program from an American network might be on.

In reality, such scenes are confined largely to cities like Peking, Shanghai, and Canton. China's peasants, the bulk of the population, remain untouched by the changes. Nevertheless at the Mao Tse-tung Memorial Hall in Peking, the "Great Helmsman"— whose body lies open to view in a glass coffin—might be seen cringing a little these days. At the far end of Tian An Men Square, atop the Gate of Heavenly Peace, Mao had proclaimed the People's Republic of China on October 1, 1949. Over the next quarter-century, he urged an unyielding "revolutionary struggle" against any encroachment of "bourgeois" Western influence. Now, less than a decade after his death, the People's Republic has Coca-Cola, tourists, and rock music.

In its effort to modernize the economy and raise the standard of living, Peking's new pragmatic leadership has rejected China's long-standing isolationism and opened its doors to the outside world. In a speech in October 1984, Deng Xiaoping said that China's isolation had kept it "impoverished, backward, and ignorant" for centuries. Beyond the principles of Western free-market capitalism, post-Mao China has looked to the outside in a variety of new ways. Slowly but steadily, it has established diplomatic and trade contacts, joint development projects, scientific and cultural exchange programs, and a growing tourist industry. Raising the 'bamboo curtain" has allowed in a host of new commodities, much-needed advanced technology, and valuable foreign currency. It has also given the Chinese people a heavy dose of Western culture, which the government has tolerated to a surprising degree. Mao may be turning in his grave, but Peking has concluded that making China "rich and strong again" depends on interaction with other countries. Said Premier Zhao Ziyang during a visit to the United States in January 1984: "China has opened its door and will never close it again."

THE BIG SHIFT

After the ice was broken in the early 1970s, U.S.-Chinese relations thawed but slowly for several years. The biggest obstacle to normalization was the Taiwan issue. Since the early 1950s, the United States had supported Taiwan as a vital strategic outpost in East Asia, an "unsinkable aircraft carrier." Washington was reluctant to cut diplomatic ties or abandon its mutual defense treaties. Peking, meanwhile, claimed that the People's Republic was the only China and that Taiwan was its legitimate possession. It insisted on a U.S.-Taiwanese break as a condition to normalization. The Shanghai Communiqué signed at the end of President Nixon's 1972 visit sidestepped the Taiwan issue, leaving it open to negotiation. That process was retarded, however, by domestic upheavals in both countries. The U.S. administration was caught up in the steadily unfolding Watergate scandal and the transition of power from President Nixon to President Ford. Peking, meanwhile, in the aftermath of the Cultural Revolution, was preoccupied by the struggle for power between Gang of Four leftists and moderate reformers. The death of Mao in 1976 and the emergence of a new leadership kept China's attention focused within, but only temporarily.

Though there were no dramatic breakthroughs during the 1972–1977 period, the trend of events was still in the direction of East-West reconciliation. The United States eased trade restrictions, reduced its commitment to Taiwan, and withdrew from Vietnam. President Ford's visit to China in December 1975 produced no important results, but it did continue the cordial relationship. China, at the same time, established or strengthened ties with Great Britain, France, Canada, the European Economic Council (EEC), Japan, and a host of other countries.

The pace of Sino-U.S. reconciliation quickened in late 1977 and 1978. Jimmy Carter was in the White House and Hua Guofeng had risen to the top in Peking. Diplomats from both sides resumed exploratory talks on normalization, with Taiwan still the main bone of contention. The big surprise came on December 15, 1978, when Washington and Peking announced in a joint communiqué that full diplomatic relations would be established. President Carter felt that the strategic importance of Taiwan was now outweighed by the benefits of full contact with the People's Republic— opening a vast commercial market and creating a strategic alliance against the Soviet Union. The United States therefore agreed to terminate official contact with Taiwan, to remove its troops from the island, and to recognize the People's Republic as the legitimate government of China. Said Carter in announcing the communiqué: "Normalization—and the expanded commercial and cultural relations that it will bring—will contribute to the well-being of our own nation, to our own national interest, and it will also enhance the stability of Asia." The statement reflected Peking's feelings precisely.

The big shift now proceeded rapidly. Deng Xiaoping, who had consolidated power in Peking, made a one-week goodwill tour of the United States in early 1979. At the conclusion of his trip, Deng and Carter signed agreements promising scientific and cultural exchange, as well as further negotiations on expanded trade. On March 1, embassies were officially opened in both countries. A trade pact was signed in July. And Vice-President Walter Mondale made a ten-day trip to China in August, agreeing to provide further commercial, financial, and developmental aid. By this time, of course, Deng's pragmatic modernization initiatives were beginning to take hold in the People's Republic.

Though the Carter administration agreed to break formal ties with Taiwan, the issue was not finally resolved. Refusing to abandon Taiwan completely, Washington did continue to supply it with "defensive" weapons and other support. Peking's dissatisfaction with that arrangement intensified when Ronald Reagan became president in 1981. Reagan had always been a strong supporter of Taiwan and an ardent opponent of the Communists. In fact, the new president entered the White House promising to restore relations with Taiwan. For a variety of reasons, primarily commercial and strategic, Reagan gradually changed his views. In August 1982, the United States and China signed a new joint communiqué: Washington pledged "to reduce gradually its sale of arms to Taiwan," while Peking would "strive for a peaceful solution to the Taiwan problem." The matter was still far from settled, but tensions were beginning to ease. Diplomatic contacts continued, trade increased, and a major sale of high-tech equipment to China was negotiated. Premier Zhao Ziyang visited Washington for three days in January 1984, signing a new series of cooperation agreements. Then in April, President Reagan made his "journey for peace" to the People's Republic, where he was greeted warmly by Deng Xiaoping and other Chinese leaders. Accords were signed on nuclear cooperation, cultural exchange, and corporate taxes. The official Chinese press said Reagan's visit "broke new ground for an enduring and steady growth in Sino-U.S. relations."

TRADE

China's new open-door policy was motivated in large measure by its need to expand and reorient foreign trade. During the 1950s, well over half of China's trade was conducted with the USSR and Soviet-bloc countries. The People's Republic imported machinery, automobiles, steel, timber, and many other commodities. The Soviets, in return, purchased vast amounts of food, textiles, and metal ores. Two-way trade between the Communist powers reached a peak of $2.1 billion in 1959. Over the next few years, however, as diplomatic and ideological differences grew wider, Sino-Soviet trade dropped of precipitously. By 1970 it had fallen to a mere $47.2 million.

In the early 1970s, with the Cultural Revolution over and relations with Moscow in a deep freeze, Peking began seeking new trading partners. It had conducted business with the Third World and other countries, but a new orientation clearly was needed. Thus, even during the last years of the Mao regime, Peking began shifting its trade policy in favor of the United States, Western Europe, Japan, and other non-Communist countries.

In the reconciliation between Peking and Washington, the first and largest strides were taken in the interests of trade. Each step forward in diplomatic and political relations coincided with, or was preceded by, progress toward increased trade contacts. The easing of U.S. trade restrictions in 1969 and 1970 led to "ping-pong diplomacy" in 1971 and President Nixon's visit to China in 1972. The period 1974–1977 saw an actual decline in Sino-U.S. trade, but this was because China was enjoying unusually good harvests and needed less imported grain. Meanwhile, the further dismantling of trade barriers gave impetus to the reconciliation process. Between 1971 and 1978, two-way trade between the two nations increased from almost nothing to more than $1 billion annually.

The big jump, of course, came with full diplomatic relations in late 1978. The United States promptly granted China "most favored nation" status, a measure that reduced U.S. tariffs on Chinese imports, made China eligible for special loans, and fostered the establishment of government and private trade offices in both countries. By 1981, two-way trade had increased five-fold again, to some $5.5 billion. Disputes over textiles and grain led to declines after 1981, but a variety of new agreements restored the upward trend in 1984.

Until the mid-1970s, China's leading export was food grain. Since then, textile products have emerged as the top commodity. Petroleum products are also increasing in importance and appears to be the major export of the future. China's greatest import needs are machinery, iron, steel, corn and wheat, and textile fibers.

In searching for new export markets and new sources for import needs, the Peking leadership has looked beyond the United States. In fact, China's largest trading partner is not the U.S., but Japan. Since the two countries established diplomatic relations in 1972, their annual two-way trade has risen to more than $10 billion annually. Japan has been China's leading supplier of machinery and equipment. Other important trade partners are Hong Kong and West Germany. Together, Japan, Hong Kong, the United States, and West Germany account for about half of China's total foreign trade.

In stark contrast to the early years of the People's

Billboard promoting a Japanese-made television. Although economic planners have begun to emphasize light industry, many consumer goods such as TVs, radios and washing machines are imported from Japan and other foreign countries. Items once not even available in China —let alone affordable—are now within reach of many ordinary citizens.

Republic, more than 90 percent of China's foreign trade today is with non-Communist countries (including many in the Third World). Nevertheless, in its zealous pursuit of modernization and economic strength, Peking has even expanded bilateral trade with the Soviet Union and Eastern Europe. Import-export with the USSR reached $1.2 billion in 1984, while trade with Hungary, Poland, Czechoslovakia, Bulgaria, and East Germany totaled some $900 million.

All in all, the opening up of China has been evidenced by a startling upsurge in foreign trade. After the Communists came to power in 1949, it took the People's Republic twenty-four years—until 1973—to reach an annual foreign trade total of $10 billion. In only one more decade, that figure had *quadrupled* to more than $40 billion.

The growth of China's overall foreign trade and its trade with the United States are charted in the tables on pages 70–71.

FOREIGN INVESTMENT

An important aspect of China's new open-door policy has been an effort to attract investments by foreign corporations and financial institutions. In addition to generating new sources of business income, this effort has helped China renovate old factories, absorb foreign technology, and learn Western management methods. The Chinese have spurred foreign investments with a variety of incentives and other special arrangements.

A key innovation in luring foreign capital has been the creation of "special economic zones" (SEZs) in several cities. The SEZs provide a favorable environment for foreign investment. Foreign firms that conduct business there enjoy inexpensive labor, cheap

CHINESE FOREIGN TRADE
1950-1984
(in millions of dollars)

Year	Total Trade	Exports by China	Imports by China	Balance
1950	$ 1,210	$ 620	$ 590	$ 30
1955	3,035	1,375	1,660	−285
1960	3,990	1,960	2,030	−70
1965	3,880	2,035	1,845	190
1970	4,340	2,095	2,245	−150
1971	4,810	2,500	2,310	190
1972	6,000	3,150	2,850	300
1973	10,300	5,075	5,225	−150
1974	14,080	6,660	7,420	−760
1975	14,575	7,180	7,395	−215
1976	13,275	7,265	6,010	1,255
1977	15,055	7,955	7,150	855
1978	21,100	9,960	11,130	−1,170
1979	29,300	13,610	15,690	−2,080
1980	37,630	18,180	19,450	−1,270
1981	43,130	21,560	21,570	−10
1982	41,005	21,475	19,530	1,945
1983	43,475	22,150	21,325	825
1984	54,276	25,760	28,516	−2,756

Sources:
CIA National Foreign Assessment Center;
U.N. Statistical Yearbook

CHINESE–U.S. TRADE
1971-1984
(in millions of dollars)

Year	Total Trade	Exports by China	Imports by China	Chinese Balance
1971	S 5	S 5	S 0	S 5
1972	96	32	64	−32
1973	805	65	740	−675
1974	934	115	819	−704
1975	462	158	304	−146
1976	337	202	135	67
1977	374	203	171	32
1978	1,142	324	818	−494
1979	2,309	592	1,717	−1,125
1980	4,807	1,058	3,749	−2,691
1981	5,498	1,895	3,603	−1,708
1982	5,196	2,284	2,912	−628
1983	4,417	2,244	2,173	71
1984	6,060	3,060	3,000	60

Sources:
U.S. Department of Commerce;
The Wall Street Journal

land, tax breaks, and other incentives. Enterprises are managed almost exclusively by foreigners, with plant managers from throughout China making visits to learn new methods. The SEZs also represent an experiment in the capitalist system; each one operates according to free-market economics. Though factories in the SEZs produce goods primarily for export, the zones may also include housing projects and even holiday resorts. Shenzhen, the fishing village that now features the Honey Lake Country Club and golf course, was one of the first four SEZs established in 1979. Since then, the Chinese government has created fourteen additional SEZs in cities on the eastern coast.

As another method of increasing foreign investment, the Chinese regime has offered contracts for "joint venture" projects. By this arrangement, the Chinese government and a foreign firm share in the development and profits of a new factory or other undertaking. A joint venture in China can take one of three basic forms: a "compensation agreement," "contract manufacturing," or direct investment. In a compensation agreement, the foreign firm sets up a plant and the government repays the cost with factory profits, periodic cash payments, or other fees. In contract manufacturing, the foreign firm merely provides the raw materials, machinery, or other essential components to a Chinese plant; the firm keeps plant profits but pays a fee to the facility. Finally, the government is now also allowing joint-venture operations in which foreign firms make a direct financial investment in a particular project and shares in actual ownership. Specific ventures can take any variation or combination of these three forms, with individually suited licensing, leasing, cooperation, compensation, or equity contracts.

The joint venture has been an effective Chinese strategy for attracting foreign capital, modernizing industry, developing new products, and tapping natural resources while at the same time dictating the terms of investment and retaining ownership and profits. By 1985, according to Peking, the policy had brought in $8 billion in foreign capital from more than 2,300 separate deals. The first joint venture with an American firm—and a glistening symbol of China's entire open-door policy—was the $75 million, 1,000-room Great Wall Hotel in Peking, built by the E-S Pacific Company. Coca-Cola (translated into Chinese as "Right for Your Mouth, Right for Your Happiness") has a bottling plant. U.S. Steel agreed to build an iron-ore processing plant. And among the many other goods and services for which China has accepted foreign investment are vehicle manufacturing, beer brewing, cigarettes, food products, photocopiers, movies and other entertainment, high-tech machinery, and electronics products. With foreign help, China plans to open its first nuclear power plant in 1988.

To fuel its industrial modernization program, Chinese planners have targeted energy production for especially aggressive joint-venture development. The nuclear power plant is just a small part of that effort. The major focus is China's offshore oil reserve, believed to be among the largest in the world. Although the People's Republic already pumps millions of gallons per day—both for domestic use and for export—the untapped reserves might allow the country to double its oil output by the year 2000. Toward that end, the Chinese government negotiated joint-venture licensing agreements with a number of foreign firms. Today some twenty-seven oil companies from nine different countries are engaged in exploratory drilling off the coast of China. Coal reserves, the nation's other major resource, are also being aggressively developed with outside assistance.

Coinciding with its efforts to attract private

Coca-Cola bottling plant in Peking

companies from abroad, the Chinese have obtained financial commitments from foreign governments, banks, and lending institutions. Between 1977 and the end of 1981, Peking lined up some $40 billion in loans and credits. Not wanting to accumulate a heavy foreign debt, the government has spent only a small fraction of the available funds. Instead, for security and long-term development, they have built up their reserves of foreign currency and maintained their lines of foreign credit. In coming years they plan to reach deeper into the coffers to purchase new technologies from abroad.

With more than one billion people, China represents a market so vast that Western businesses and banks are willing to make great concessions just to gain a foothold. The Peking leadership has offered lucrative profit opportunities, but it has also moved forward cautiously. It has developed only those goods and services that it deems necessary for the country's economic progress. The Chinese have not forgotten the centuries of humiliation and oppression suffered at the hands of foreigners, and they insist on absolute "equality and mutual benefit" in all business transactions. Foreign investment will continue to be pursued, but in a measured fashion and only in the best interests of China. Said one Western observer: "The Chinese have rediscovered that they are the center of the world. They have put themselves in the position of being courted by everyone."

TOURISM AND
EXCHANGE PROGRAMS

The door to China has been opened not only to presidents, diplomats, and businessmen. Foreign tourists are invited in to see the sights of ancient Zhong Guo and the changes taking place in the modern People's

Republic. The government has made a concerted effort to develop the tourist industry as another source of foreign currency. Through joint ventures, it has constructed several first-class, Western-style hotels. It has improved air travel and train accommodations for foreigners. And it has trained thousands of guides to escort tourist groups through the country. While ordinary Chinese are not usually permitted in tourist hotels and other facilities, the government encourages them to show hospitality and friendliness in any contact with foreigners. And finally, China remains one of the most fascinating and inexpensive travel spots in the world for Western tourists. As a result, more than one million foreigners, about one-fifth of them from the United States, visited China in 1984. They spent a total of more than $1 billion during their stays. Both figures are expected to increase significantly in coming years.

Chinese citizens are not normally allowed to leave the country; few could afford foreign travel anyway. However, a growing number of students and scientists have been sent abroad for special training. From 1975 to 1984, some 18,500 of them had been sent to study in 54 different countries. More than 10,000 have gone to the United States alone. In addition, thousands of athletes, entertainers, and diplomatic personnel have had the opportunity to see life outside the People's Republic. All those who travel abroad bring back new ideas and vivid impressions which their families, friends, and neighbors are eager to hear about.

CHOPSTICKS
AND LIPSTICK

The advent of a consumer-based economy and the influx of Western culture have come abruptly to the

People's Republic of China. In less than one decade, Deng's pragmatic policies have set the "poor man of Asia" on a course of prosperity and strength. The new open-door policy has yanked China from decades of isolation and thrust it into the commercial, cultural, and political affairs of the world community. All the exposure to foreign ways has brought startling change to everyday life in China, from medicine and music to fashion and food.

The Chinese people have embraced the new opportunities and new freedoms with obvious enthusiasm. Nevertheless, following so closely on the heels of Mao's grim garrison state, the world of Coca-Cola and electric music has been disorienting to many Chinese, especially the older generations. Moreover, for a civilization so ancient, so proud of its heritage, and so bound by tradition, the rapid cultural transformation has conflicted with some deep-seated attitudes and values. China today is exploring a strange, uncharted sea, and it is clearly following a westerly course. The sailing, however, has not been all smooth.

The new thinking of Peking's leadership was never more clearly evidenced than in a speech by party leader Hu Yaobang in December 1984. A strong proponent of Westernization, Hu called on the Chinese people to throw away one of the most familiar and most traditional items in their daily lives—chopsticks. Said Hu: "We should sit around the table and eat Chinese food in the Western style, that is, each from his own plate." Hu suggested that the changeover might reduce contagious disease, but the spirit of his message went far deeper than that. "Eating from the big pot" is a common Chinese expression for the group and family ethic. Eating with chopsticks from bowls in the middle of the table reflects the deeply ingrained Chinese spirit of communal sharing. Hu's call for eating "in the Western style, each from his own plate" thus represented an attack against the group ethic and an exhortation to individualism. But while the speech was a strong refutation of Maoist egalitarianism, it also contradicted an ancient and fundamental Chinese way of thinking. "Eating from the big pot"— with chopsticks—will not be discarded so quickly.

In other aspects of daily life, however, the Chinese have appeared willing, even anxious, to dispense with traditional values and socialist principles. Self-sacrifice and self-effacement have given way to self-identity and self-interest. The drab, loose-fitting tunics of Mao's era are being replaced by narrow-waisted dresses and tailored suits. Modeling schools and beauty contests have come to Shanghai and Peking. Cosmetics sales are booming in department stores throughout the country. Lipstick and mascara, considered "decadent and bourgeois" only a few years ago, are now a common indulgence of young Chinese women.

While it continues to promote such Western values as self-sufficiency and individual responsibility, the government is being careful not to let things go too far. In October 1983, the Communist Party Central Committee—perhaps seeing too much long hair and too many "USA" T-shirts—retreated from its permissive posture and launched a heavy propaganda campaign against "spiritual pollution and cultural contamination." It called for resistance to "obscene, barbarous, or reactionary things" and, in a move reminiscent of the Cultural Revolution, put thousands of workers through weeks of "ideological study."

The "spiritual pollution" campaign lasted only a few months, but the party has tried to keep some control over the unwanted aspects of Westernization. It reserves harsh penalties for the new class of Chinese criminal who lives off the new private sector by smuggling, stealing, and other "nonproductive" activities. Meanwhile, the official press continues to decry "frivolous and depraved drama and literature." As one 1984 headline put it: "We Want to Import Japanese Computers, Not Striptease."

Peking's open-door policy has brought vast change to the economic and cultural life of the People's Republic. The government has aggressively pursued foreign capital and actively promoted Western ways of thinking. Yet, always in search of an independent course, China has moved forward with circumspection. In trade and commerce, it has restricted its dealings to goods and services that are in the nation's own best interest. In cultural affairs, it has resisted change that does not promote a better quality of life. While the general direction of change is clear, there remains some uncertainty—among the leaders and the people alike—as to how much change is desirable.

The same search for an independent course, the same circumspection, and the same uncertainty have been seen in China's ever-shifting foreign policies.

Chapter 5
Swings in the Pendulum

In its ongoing quest for prosperity and strength, China has cut a winding path through the twentieth century. In a bewildering series of ideological twists and political turns, its domestic policy makers have swung crazily between traditionalism and modernization, restraint and development, repression and liberalism. From the end of the Qing Dynasty to the Nationalist government of Chiang Kai-shek to the Communist People's Republic, the Chinese people have endured innumerable shifts and countershifts in political, economic, and cultural life. Since 1949 alone, they have witnessed the Hundred Flowers Campaign, the Great Leap Forward, the Cultural Revolution, the Four Modernizations, the Spiritual Pollution Campaign, and other swings to the left or right.

Modern China has demonstrated an equally ambivalent attitude toward the outside world. Its changing posture has reflected a continuing "debate" between two groups of Chinese statesmen. Some, like Mao Tse-tung, have believed that China should remain closed to the outside world and pursue a course of radical self-reliance. Others, like Deng Xiaoping, have contended that China must open up and learn from foreign ways. While generally aloof from the world community and fundamentally suspicious of other cultures, China has come out of its isolationist shell at various times. As early as the 1890s, a popular reform movement was urging modernization along Western lines. In the 1930s, Chiang Kai-shek called for similar innovation in industry, science, and management. And under the current pragmatic leadership, China has once again ventured onto the international scene.

The swings in Chinese foreign policy have been especially pronounced since 1949. Unable or unwilling to divorce itself completely from world politics, the Communist leadership has moved China back and forth between the two major poles in modern global affairs—the United States and the Soviet Union. These shifts have occurred roughly every ten years. During the 1950s, the fledgling People's Republic maintained close and friendly relations with the USSR, while the U.S. was shut out. The pendulum began to swing in the 1960s, as the Sino-Soviet rift grew wider. By the 1970s, ties were being forged with Washington, and Moscow was in the cold. Finally, the 1980s have seen a clear movement back toward the center. For despite China's opening up to U.S. trade and investment, it has held back from a close alliance and insisted on an "independent foreign policy." In defining its own brand of Communism and seeking greater influence on the world scene, China's most recent diplomatic strategy has been to take a "nonaligned" middle ground between the two superpowers.

THE STRATEGIC
TRIANGLE

The major trends and developments in international politics today revolve closely around the strategic interests of the United States, the Soviet Union, and the People's Republic of China. For the past three decades or more, events in virtually every corner of the world have been affected by the dynamics of this great power triangle. China's influence within the triangle derives less from its nuclear arsenal, which has not nearly kept pace with that of the Americans or Soviets, than from its economic and military *potential*. Its ability to swing from one side to the other gives it enormous sway in the global rivalry between the U.S. and USSR. Its shifting alignments from decade to decade have reflected the ups and downs of U.S.-Soviet relations, the apparent intentions of Washington and Moscow, and Peking's determination of how best to take advantage.

Shared Communist ideals, economic and military aid, and the defense of Asia against "bourgeois imperialism" had Peking leaning heavily toward its Moscow comrades during the 1950s. The United States —locked in Cold War with the Soviets, fighting a real war in Korea, and giving military support to Taiwan— was considered an ideological villain and a strategic threat. China's position in the great power triangle underwent radical change over the next decade as ties with Moscow weakened, Soviet troops were building along the border, the Korean War was drifting into history, and overtures began to emanate from Washington. By the mid-1970s, China was leaning heavily toward the United States in a common front against Soviet domination.

Today Peking refers to these two periods in its diplomatic history as the two "lean-tos." It believes that China tilted too far both toward the Russians in the 1950s *and* toward the Americans in the 1970s. Now, while it continues to be closer with Washington than with Moscow, it has sought to restore a measure of its long-cherished autonomy. China's "independent foreign policy" of the 1980s has resulted in large part from heightened tensions between the U.S. and Soviet Union, as well as from several moderating factors in its separate relations with Washington and Moscow.

The nuclear arms race between the United States and the Soviet Union, combined with the bitter verbal attacks between the White House and the Kremlin, has been a source of deep consternation throughout the world. China has shared this concern, but the situation has also provided it a new freedom in its foreign policy. Peking has refused to take sides in the contest, but it remains secure of American help in the event of a nuclear attack by the Soviets. With President Reagan taking an aggressive stand against the Kremlin, Peking has let him carry the burden of keeping the Soviets in check. The Chinese are in a position, according to one diplomat, to "sit on the mountain and watch the tigers fight." In a delicate balancing act, Peking has set limits on its ties with Washington, while improving relations with Moscow. Because of intriguing changes in the strategic triangle, it has let the pendulum swing closer to middle ground without jeopardizing its security in the nuclear age.

China's diplomatic relations with the United States have never advanced quite so far as its trade and commercial relations. By the late 1970s, the important political breakthroughs had been made and the vital diplomatic contacts had been established: official recognition had been exchanged, embassies had been opened, a series of bilateral agreements had been signed, and students and tourists were flowing back and forth. During the 1980s, however, even as U.S. trade and investment were increasing, diplomatic relations remained at arm's length. Perhaps the first sign was Peking's refusal to accept U.S. military assistance, a clear signal of its desire to remain "non-aligned." Beyond that, there were still fundamental political and cultural differences between the two countries. While Chinese exchange students were bringing back valuable technical expertise, the Peking leadership was leery of exposing too many Chinese to American democracy and material comforts. Already it was having trouble controlling the spread of American culture, and already there had been defections.* Perhaps most importantly, the Taiwan question remained a thorn in the side of China's leaders. The United States was continuing to sell arms to the Nationalist government there, and President Reagan, despite his new outlook, refused to abandon Taiwan altogether. For all these reasons, and still others, U.S.-Chinese diplomatic relations have advanced little since the initial gains of the 1970s.

In the meantime, China's perception of the Soviet Union has changed in important ways during the 1980s. First, it has concluded that the Russians probably will not launch an invasion after all. The Soviets have long maintained a vast and sophisticated military force along the border, but no large-scale invasion has ever materialized. Moreover, Moscow has turned its attention to other, more pressing foreign concerns: its war in Afghanistan, Poland, the Middle East, missile deployment in Europe, and the arms competition with the United States. The fierce anti-Soviet posture being taken by Washington would itself quell any Kremlin ideas of invading China. In addition, mounting economic difficulties in the USSR and several changes in that nation's leadership have made a move into China even more remote.

---

* Among the defectors was tennis star Hu Na in July 1982. When the United States granted her political asylum in April 1983, Peking issued an angry protest and canceled nineteen cultural and sports exchange programs.

As the Chinese have become less fearful of the Soviets, they have also seen the present and long-term advantages of closer ties with Moscow. The aggressive modernization program begun by Peking can succeed only in a peaceful environment, without the fear of war and without heavy defense spending by the government. With actual Soviet assistance, the program would stand an even greater chance of reaching its goals. In terms of China's diplomatic strategy, closer contact with Moscow would also remind Washington of Peking's autonomy in world affairs. Since it officially declared its "independent foreign policy" in 1982, the People's Republic has therefore established new contacts with the USSR. First, after a Soviet call for "normalization and a gradual improvement in relations," Peking agreed to a series of high-level talks. Then trade began to increase, and Chinese students began appearing in Moscow. Finally, in December 1984, Peking welcomed Soviet Premier Ivan Arkhipov on a nine-day visit; he became the highest-ranking Kremlin official to visit the People's Republic in fifteen years. Arkhipov's visit culminated in a series of accords on scientific and technological exchange, increased trade, and Soviet assistance in the modernization of Chinese factories.

The actual normalization talks between China and the USSR have made little progress since 1982, and the prospects for any major reconciliation appear weak. Having discarded the Soviet model and pursued its own brand of Communism for more than twenty years, the People's Republic is unwilling to return to the unbalanced alliance of the 1950s. For the time being, the two Communist giants have aired their differences and reduced the level of tension. As for normalized relations, the Chinese have presented Moscow with three absolute preconditions: 1) to reduce the number of Soviet troops along the Chinese border; 2) to withdraw Soviet forces from Afghanistan, where they are considered a threat to the neighboring People's Republic and its ally, Pakistan; and 3) to stop supporting Vietnam's occupation of Cambodia, whose present puppet government overthrew a Chinese-supported regime in 1978.

SECURITY IN ASIA

The three conditions presented to Moscow reflect China's interest in promoting security—and Chinese influence—in its own backyard of Asia. The policies of the People's Republic toward its Asian neighbors have been determined over several decades by the often convulsive chains of events within individual countries, by the roles and relationships of the United States and Soviet Union, and by its own interests in promoting regional peace and stability. Because Moscow today poses the greater security threat throughout the continent, Peking's interests and policies generally coincide with those of Washington. Nevertheless, China's "nonaligned" position and America's military history in Asia (not to mention the Taiwan issue) have caused disagreements.

Among the deepest concerns of China today is the ongoing political and military upheaval in Southeast Asia. In the past twenty years, no other region of the world has been more politically volatile, more ravaged by war, or more directly affected by the United States, the Soviet Union, and China. At the center of all the conflict have been Vietnam, which lies on China's southern frontier, and Cambodia.

China's military support of Hanoi went back to the Vietnamese Communist's war with France in the early 1950s. The flow of arms and other materiel continued through the U.S. involvement of the 1960s and 1970s, which included the bombing of supply trails and Communist strongholds in Cambodia. After the withdrawal of U.S. troops in 1973, the Communist regime in North Vietnam, with considerable aid from the Soviet Union, renewed its armed offensive against democratic South Vietnam. China's relations with Hanoi soured in 1975, when North Vietnamese forces achieved final victory over the South.

Peking turned to the new Communist regime of Pol Pot in Cambodia as its major ally in the region. In April 1975, Pol Pot had overthrown the government of Lon Nol, which the United States had supported. Armed by the Chinese, Pol Pot carried out one of the bloodiest political campaigns in history, exterminating at least two million Cambodians. But Pol Pot also got into conflict with Communist Vietnam, and that proved disastrous. In late 1978, Vietnam launched a major invasion of Cambodia and overran the country within two weeks. Hanoi promptly installed a puppet regime, headed by Heng Samrin.

China reacted to the loss of Cambodia by invading northern Vietnam in February 1979. Although its troops were withdrawn three weeks later, there was no settlement between the two countries. Border skirmishing has continued to the present day. The Soviet Union remains a close ally of Vietnam and backs the puppet regime in Cambodia, while China supports a Cambodian guerrilla movement to overthrow that regime. The United States, meanwhile, still officially recognizes the Pol Pot regime. Because of Pol Pot's record of tyranny and America's own memories of the Vietnam War, however, Washington is not involved in Southeast Asian affairs as much as Peking would like. All in all, a grim history has left a complex situation which the People's Republic views as a serious danger to regional stability and its own security.

China's demand of Soviet military withdrawal from

Afghanistan reflects similar concern over security in south-central Asia. The Soviet occupation of Afghanistan in late 1979 was regarded in Peking as a criminal act which typified Moscow's corruption of the Marxist-Leninist ideal. The continued presence of Soviet troops there is seen as a further act of aggression with the specific purpose of containing the People's Republic. Afghanistan shares a short border with China and a very long one with Pakistan, China's closest ally in the region. The Soviet presence in Afghanistan, Peking feels, gives Moscow a dangerous advantage in the decades-long struggle for strategic control of south-central Asia.

That contest can be traced to the Sino-Soviet split of the 1960s and Moscow's subsequent efforts to win India as a regional ally. Peking, in turn, provided economic and military assistance to the nations immediately surrounding India. In 1971, fortified by a major defense pact and a twenty-year friendship treaty with the USSR, India invaded Pakistan—which was supported by China. The Indian forces easily defeated the smaller Pakistani units and ordered a cease-fire two weeks later. The result was a dismemberment of Pakistan and the creation of a new nation, Bangladesh. In the wake of its loss, China clung ever more tightly to Pakistan as its strategic foothold in the region. Along with a Soviet naval buildup in the Indian Ocean, however, the occupation of Afghanistan tipped the overall balance precariously in favor of Moscow.

Since 1979, China's strategic position in the area has improved marginally. India has edged away from the Soviet Union and forged modest new ties with the United States and China. Still, Peking remains critical of the United States (especially the former Carter administration) for not taking stronger action against the Soviet occupation of Afghanistan.

The shifts in the strategic triangle over recent

decades are nowhere better demonstrated than in Korea, located on a northeastern peninsula of the Chinese mainland. In 1945, at the end of World War II, the United States occupied South Korea and the Soviet Union occupied North Korea. Under U.N. supervision, a democratic government was elected in the South, and the Republic of Korea was declared in 1948. Later that year, under Soviet supervision, the Democratic People's Republic of Korea—a Communist regime—was established in the North. Both sides claimed sovereignty over all Korea. By mid-1949, the U.S. and USSR had withdrawn their occupation troops, but by mid-1950 war had broken out between North and South Korea. U.N. forces led by the United States joined the fighting on behalf of South Korea; Chinese Communist forces fought for the North. The Korean War lasted three full years, until the armistice of July 1953.

Today North Korea remains Communist, and South Korea democratic. China and the Soviet Union both support the North and refuse to formally recognize the South. Nevertheless, the Chinese and Soviets remain regional rivals, pursuing a costly competition for the favor of the North Korean regime. For the sake of stability and security in East Asia, Peking has also encouraged reconciliation talks between the North and South. Most recently, the Chinese have increased trade with South Korea and expressed interest in establishing other informal ties. Thus, Peking's position with regard to Korea stands somewhere between that of Moscow and Washington—a middle ground. Its official policy is aligned with the Kremlin's, but—three decades after the Korean War—its real interests in the area have more in common with those of the United States.

In its efforts to promote regional stability, build a common front against the Soviets, and develop new trade and commercial contacts, the People's

Republic has cultivated closer relations with other non-Communist neighbors in Asia. The most notable of these is Japan. After centuries of war and enmity, the two countries have realized important benefits from friendly relations. As China's largest trading partner, Japan represents a valuable asset to Peking's economic development program. As the world's most populous nation, China represents a vast new market for Japanese products. And like Peking, Tokyo worries about Soviet intervention in East Asia; the new relationship strengthens the security of both nations. For similar reasons, China has also sought stronger ties with the Association of Southeast Asian Nations (ASEAN)—Indonesia, Malaysia, the Philippines, Singapore, and Thailand. ASEAN opposes the Soviet-backed Vietnamese regime in Cambodia, and the individual ASEAN countries represent potentially valuable economic partners.

THE THIRD WORLD

China's "independent foreign policy" was formally announced at the 12th Communist Party Congress in September 1982. The declaration marked the official end of Peking's strategic alignment with the United States and the beginning of its new emphasis on relations with the Third World. The actual shift, however, had been clearly evidenced since the late 1970s, when Sino-U.S. diplomatic relations began hitting roadblocks. China's orientation toward the Third World was signaled in a speech by Deng Xiaoping at the U.N. General Assembly in April 1979. Said Deng:

The United States and the Soviet Union make up the First World. The developed countries between the two make up the Second World.

The developing countries in Asia, Africa, Latin America, and other regions make up the Third World. . . . China belongs to the Third World. The Chinese government and people firmly support all oppressed peoples and oppressed nations in their struggle to win or defend national independence, develop the economy, and oppose colonialism, imperialism, and hegemonism by the superpowers. This is our bounden internationalist duty.

Since 1949, China's relations with developing nations in Africa, Latin America, and the Middle East have followed the same swinging pendulum as its relations with the Soviet Union and United States. During the Sino-Soviet alliance of the 1950s, China generally supported Russian causes in Africa and maintained good relations with Soviet allies in the Middle East (principally Egypt) and Latin America. After breaking with Moscow in the 1960s, Peking began opposing Soviet Third World interests and promoting its own. In Africa it supported "wars of national liberation" and financed huge aid projects in Tanzania and Zambia. In the Middle East it sided with such radical governments as Algeria, Syria, and Yemen. And in Latin America it supported anti-Soviet regimes and ended friendly relations with Cuba. Then during the 1970s, as it leaned toward the United States, Peking neglected its own Third World interests and sided with those of Washington. In Africa it aligned itself with the United States against Cuban- and Soviet-armed troops in Angola. In the Middle East it moderated its policies and helped serve U.S. peace efforts by restoring support for Egypt (which had long since broken with Moscow). And in Latin America it generally went along with U.S. policy.

In the 1980s, Peking's "independent foreign policy"

has become a catchphrase for its renewed identification with the Third World. China has taken a variety of steps to strengthen old ties and establish new ones among the world's poorer nations. Diplomatic contact is being expanded, assistance programs are being revived, educational and technical training programs are being offered to increasing numbers of Third World visitors, and regional policies are being reshaped to oppose superpower "hegemonism and expansionism." Although the People's Republic is not an official member of the Nonaligned Movement, it has expressed strong support for the organization's objectives. As the United Nations has become increasingly dominated by Third World members, China has taken a more active role and has raised its financial commitment. And in virtually every part of the world, the People's Republic has championed the cause of developing nations with material or verbal support.

Outside of Asia, China's efforts to gain influence among developing nations and to promote Third World cooperation have been most intensive in Africa. Soon after the 1982 foreign policy pronouncement, Peking moved to settle differences with the now Marxist government of Angola. It also established diplomatic relations with such countries as Lesotho and the Ivory Coast, while making informal contact with several other African states. In December 1982, Premier Zhao Ziyang began a month-long, eleven-nation tour of the continent; it was the first visit by a top Chinese leader since 1964. During his tour, Zhao signed agreements for a $37 million loan to Zimbabwe, for the cancellation of a $100 million debt owed by Zaire, and for an increase in the purchase of exports from Kenya. At every stop he voiced strong criticism of both Soviet and U.S. behavior.

In the Middle East, closer to home and more vulnerable to Soviet influence, China has retained its overall pro-U.S. posture. During his African tour, Zhao made a major sale of fighter planes to Egypt and recognized Israel's right to exist. Nevertheless, in opposition to U.S. policy, China pledged support to Yasir Arafat and the Palestine Liberation Organization, a member of the Nonaligned Movement. It has also refused to grant full diplomatic recognition to Israel, even though Israel recognized the People's Republic as early as 1950.

In Latin America, where Chinese strategic and economic interests are remote, Peking generally keeps hands off. It is reluctant to interfere in the U.S. backyard and continues to criticize Soviet and Cuban activities. Still, Chinese weapons have been reported in El Salvador, and Peking has issued strong verbal attacks against U.S. policy in Central America, especially in Nicaragua.

Not to be ignored in China's new orientation toward the world community is the extent to which Peking holds back from the Third World and the ways in which it remains tied to the West. For even as it courts the Third World and proclaims its support for the cause of "oppressed peoples," China conducts only a small portion—less than 10 percent— of its overall world trade with developing nations. And even as it refers to U.S. "exploitation and imperialism," Peking remains aligned with U.S. policy in critical areas of the world. With all its substantive and rhetorical support of the Third World, the Chinese leadership fully recognizes two limiting factors on its new foreign policy approach. First, the success of its domestic modernization campaign will depend on strong economic ties with the developed nations of the West. Second, security against the Soviet Union and stability in Asia are vitally served by strategic cooperation with the United States.

In sum, the pendulum of Chinese foreign policy has swung noticeably toward the center in the 1980s, while still leaning toward the United States. To the extent that Peking has established an "independent foreign policy" and assumed a leadership role in the Third World, it has satisfied some long-held national yearnings. Having broken from the Soviet sphere and set some distance from the United States, China has reaffirmed its deeply cherished autonomy. As a champion of the Third World, it views itself as a leader among nations—a modern Middle Kingdom.

Still to be fulfilled are two other long-held ambitions of the Communist Chinese leadership—the recoveries of Taiwan and Hong Kong.

Chapter 6
Taiwan and Hong Kong

Since the rule of Emperor Qin Shi Huang Di in the 3rd century B.C., China has clung resolutely—at times desperately—to the idea of a unified sovereign nation. Through centuries of invasion and foreign rule, the desire to make China whole again became a deeply ingrained national aspiration, a compulsion of many generations of Chinese leaders. Even today, nearly four decades after Mao Tse-tung rallied the Chinese masses under the red flag of Communism, the goal of "reunification" remains very much alive in the high circles of Peking. Never forgotten were the humiliating loss of Hong Kong to Britain in the mid-nineteenth century or the breaking loose of Chiang Kai-shek's Nationalist government to Taiwan in 1949. The recoveries of Hong Kong and Taiwan would restore full unity to China and complete its long struggle for national "liberation." Whatever the success or failure of his economic and political reforms, Deng Xiaoping (or any other Chinese leader) would earn an important place in history for managing to get back either one of them.

Taiwan and Hong Kong today are thriving capitalist enclaves that little relish the thought of a Communist takeover. In both cases, Peking has promised special autonomy under "peaceful reunification." Because of past and present circumstances, however, the two areas face very different prospects. While Taiwan remains far out of the grasp of Peking, Hong Kong is within tantalizing reach.

TAIWAN

The Republic of China on the island of Taiwan lies approximately 100 miles (160 km) off the east coast of the Chinese mainland. After the arrival of Chiang Kai-shek and his defeated Kuomintang forces in 1949, the United States (and later Japan) invested heavily in the island's economy. On the strength of rice, sugar, and other agricultural products, as well as textiles and electronics manufacturing, the island's capitalist system brought steady growth and increasing prosperity. Today the 19.5 million residents of Taiwan enjoy one of the highest standards of living in Asia. In the area of government and politics, the Kuomintang remains the dominant force in Taipei (the capital city). Chiang Ching-kuo, the eldest son of Chiang Kai-shek, began taking over the reigns of power in the early 1970s, becoming premier and chairman of the Kuomintang. In 1978 he was elected to a six-year term as president, and in 1984 he was reelected, both times without real opposition. While the system of government is nominally democratic, having a formal constitution and an elected legislature, the Kuomintang exerts firm political control. Freedom is limited, and opposition is dealt with harshly. Government censorship is among the strictest in the world.

Technically, Taiwan is not an independent nation but a province of China. The question is: *whose* China? The civil war that brought the Communists to power in Peking and forced the Nationalists to Taiwan was never formally ended. Chiang Kai-shek and the Kuomintang never surrendered their sovereignty. Thus, just as Peking regards Taiwan as an official province of the People's Republic, so Taipei lays claim to the entire mainland as part of the Nationalist Republic. In fact, the Taiwanese leadership attaches the same importance to reunification as Peking does, but on the condition that the mainland give up Communism and recognize the Nationalists as the legitimate rulers of all China.

In the forum of international politics, the argument over who represents the real China clearly is being won by the Communists. Among all the nations of the world, only a very few still withhold formal recognition of the People's Republic and maintain full diplomatic relations with Taiwan. Indeed, the United States in 1978 was one of the last nations to establish formal ties with Peking and sever them with Taipei. In 1971 the United Nations had voted overwhelmingly to oust the Nationalist Republic and to seat the People's Republic. Even in the Olympic Games, the People's Republic now competes under the name of China. (The Nationalists also send a team, but under the name of Taiwan.)

This nearly universal backing of Peking has been based less on any moral or legal claims to legitimacy than on several more practical considerations. To developing nations, the People's Republic is both a protector and an economic benefactor. To the West and Japan, it represents a staggering new market and a shared strategic interest against the Soviet Union. Finally, the fact remains that the Communists have controlled the vast majority of Chinese territory for nearly forty years.

Nevertheless, in the United States (and in other countries), the debate goes on over the two-China situation. Pro-Taiwanese lobby groups and many politicians continue to contend that Washington was wrong to abandon its long-time Nationalist allies. The withdrawal of support in 1978, they maintain, undermined U.S. credibility throughout the world. Even worse, the repeal of the mutual defense treaty in 1979 made Taiwan vulnerable to Communist aggression. What had happened to the pledge of making Taiwan an "unsinkable aircraft carrier"? On the other side of the coin, it is argued that the mainland Chinese have shown no threat against Taiwan in years and that the island continues to flourish. Washington, it is contended, serves important commercial and strategic interests by siding with Peking. Moreover, Taipei's authoritarian regime does not deserve U.S. support anyway. Finally, the Taiwan Relations Act of 1979 (passed shortly after formal recognition of the People's Republic) promised friendly if unofficial relations with Taipei, as well as the sale of "defensive" weapons. Since its passage, U.S. arms deals and other contacts have irked Peking and served notice of Washington's continuing concern for Taiwanese security.

If the mainland Chinese had hoped that the United States might help them get back Taiwan, they were promptly set straight. And if Peking harbored any lingering notions of a forceful takeover, it began to see a more sensible course. In the 1980s, China's pragmatic leadership has begun to establish its own unofficial contacts with Taipei and to develop indirect trade relations. Conducted through Hong Kong and Japan, two-way trade between the People's Republic and Taiwan is now estimated at several hundred million dollars a year. Ever hopeful of bringing Taiwan back into the fold, Peking in September 1981 proposed reunification talks and offered the Nationalists "posts of leadership" in the united government. According to the nine-point program drawn up by the Communists,

Taiwan would become a "special administrative zone." Its social and economic systems would be preserved, its armed forces would remain intact, and its relations with other countries would not be jeopardized. The Nationalists immediately rejected the overture as a propaganda ploy to undermine Taiwan's morale and to lure it into Communist subjugation. Denouncing the Peking regime as tyrannical, Chiang Ching-kuo held firmly to the position that the only way to solve the two-China problem was to eliminate Communism. That, of course, was the least likely prospect of all.

Despite the priority that both governments place on a united China, the chances for reunification thus appear slim—and growing slimmer. In Peking, the yearning to win back Taiwan is strongest among older officials who remember when the Nationalists broke away. The younger officials who will replace them in coming years seem to have less of an emotional stake in the whole matter. And the same process appears to be taking place on Taiwan. Native-born islanders as well as the children of former mainlanders do not seem to share their elders' deep desire to oust the Communists. As for reincorporation into the People's Republic, Taiwan simply does not trust Peking's promises and sees little to gain anyway. While Taiwan has few formal diplomatic ties, it remains strategically secure and economically prosperous on its own.

The two-China situation therefore seems likely to continue in the foreseeable future. Though new contacts may be forged, the Nationalists and Communists can be expected to remain autonomous rivals for some time to come. And, barring some drastic turn of events or unanticipated shift in policy, Washington will continue its unofficial support of Taipei. That alone will create an obstacle to closer U.S.-Chinese relations. Taiwan is proving to be something of an "unsinkable aircraft carrier" after all.

Not far away, meanwhile, a very different story is being played out.

HONG KONG

Located on the southeastern coast of the Chinese mainland in the South China Sea, Hong Kong (which means "fragrant harbor") is a 400-sq-mile (1,036-sq-km) British colony which includes Hong Kong Island, the Kowloon Peninsula, the New Territories, and some 235 offshore islands. About 90 percent of the total area is accounted for by the New Territories, which lies on the mainland about 85 miles (137 km) south of Canton. Kowloon, a peninsula on the southern end of the New Territories, is the colony's major industrial area. South again from Kowloon, across a bustling harbor, lies Hong Kong Island. The center of government and commerce is the capital city of Victoria, located on Hong Kong Island. A large majority of Hong Kong's 5.5 million residents (about 90 percent of whom are ethnic Chinese) live around the harbor in Victoria and Kowloon.

The fine harbor facilities, well-developed shipping services, absence of customs duties, and efficient support industries long ago established Hong Kong as the center of East-West trade. Since the influx of cheap, abundant labor from China after World War II, Hong Kong has emerged as a major exporter of light industrial goods, especially textiles. Its thriving capitalist system is perhaps the closest thing to a pure free-market economy in the world. At present the colony is administered by a governor representing the British crown, assisted by a local Executive Council and Legislative Council; ultimate authority lies with the British Parliament. Because of an agreement reached with China in the late 1800s, however,

Britain's control of Hong Kong is nearing expiration. The coming years will see some basic changes, at least in the form of government.

The territories that now make up Hong Kong were under Chinese sovereignty for more than 2,000 years, beginning in about 200 B.C. In the mid-1800s, however, when strained trade relations between China and Great Britain erupted in the Opium War, British expeditionary forces occupied the then barren island of Hong Kong. Under the Treaty of Nanking, which officially ended the Opium War in 1842, China was forced to cede (give up sovereignty of) Hong Kong Island to the British crown. In another humiliation to the Chinese, the 1860 Treaty of Peking ceded the Kowloon Peninsula and several islands to Great Britain. Finally, in 1898, as a result of international tension in the Far East and the need to protect Hong Kong harbor, Britain secured a lease of the New Territories. According to the lease, this largest part of Hong Kong would remain a British colony for a period of ninety-nine years.

Japanese forces attacked Hong Kong on the same day that they were bombing Pearl Harbor in December 1941. Britain surrendered its colony later that month. After regaining control at the end of World War II, the British oversaw an astonishing growth and transformation of the Hong Kong economy. With the Communist takeover of China in 1949, however, the government in Peking began insisting that the "unequal" treaties giving control of Hong Kong to Britain were invalid. The People's Republic began pressing its claim to rightful sovereignty over the entire territory.

Peking's claim was largely ignored, but with each passing decade the expiration of Britain's lease on the New Territories loomed closer. British control would end on June 30, 1997, and the New Territories would revert to Chinese sovereignty; the remaining 10 percent of Hong Kong would be severely crippled.

The prospect of Communist rule led to declining confidence in Hong Kong's future, reflected in a steady outflow of capital, a reduction in new investments, a gradual drop in stock prices, and a rise in the number of emigration applications.

The opening of Chinese-British negotiations in September 1982 did little to allay the fears of Hong Kong. By the following summer, the talks were still at an impasse. Seeking to preserve the social and economic freedom of Hong Kong, the British team wanted a detailed agreement spelling out the exact terms of the transfer. The Chinese were willing to make Hong Kong a "special administrative zone," but they insisted on a broad, general agreement. Peking was in a position to accept or reject any proposal, and they refused to be bound by any narrow set of restrictions. Growing impatient with the British position, Peking finally issued an ultimatum: unless an agreement were reached by September 1984, it would announce its own plans for Hong Kong.

During the first half of 1984, the fears of the people of Hong Kong were deepened by several events. In March, one of the colony's oldest and largest trading companies announced that it was moving its headquarters to Bermuda. In April, Britain announced that it would relinquish all of Hong Kong when its lease on the New Territories expires. And in May, Deng Xiaoping declared that China would station troops in Hong Kong after 1997. With each new development, the Hong Kong stock market and the value of the Hong Kong dollar fell precipitously. By the summer of 1984, with the Chinese deadline approaching, the atmosphere in the colony was extremely tense.

Then, on August 1, after nineteen rounds of talks, British Foreign Secretary Sir Geoffrey Howe announced that an agreement had been reached. For fifty years after 1997, Sir Geoffrey said, the accord would "provide for the preservation of all the rights and freedoms which the people of Hong Kong now enjoy." All of Hong Kong would be turned over to the Chinese, but, as a "special administrative zone," it would retain a high degree of autonomy for fifty years. After the draft agreement was initialed by both sides in late September, the treaty was ratified by the Hong Kong Legislative Council in mid-October and by the British Parliament in early December. (China's nominal parliament, the National People's Congress, gave its pro-forma ratification in 1985.) The official signing ceremony was held in Peking on December 19, 1984. The final document was signed by Premier Zhao Ziyang of the People's Republic and by Prime Minister Margaret Thatcher of Great Britain.

The full agreement established the kind of detailed framework that the British had sought. It enumerated the rights and freedoms of the Hong Kong people; stipulated the organization of the Hong Kong government; and defined the local authority in trade, commerce, transportation, and foreign relations. Specifically, it guaranteed freedom "of speech, of the press, of assembly, of association, of travel, of movement, of correspondence, of strike, of choice of occupation, of academic research, and of religious belief." Private ownership, of both property and business, was similarly protected.

According to the agreement, Hong Kong's present legal and judicial system would be maintained for the fifty-year period. The government and legislature would be made up of local inhabitants. Hong Kong's status as a free port, a separate customs territory, and an international financial center would be assured. Its markets for foreign exchange, securities, gold, and futures would continue to conduct business. Under the name Hong Kong, China, the territory would be allowed to maintain economic and cultural relations with other countries. Peking would not levy taxes on Hong Kong, but it would station troops there—on the condition that they do not interfere in Hong Kong's internal affairs. After 1997, all ethnic Chinese in Hong Kong would become citizens of the People's Republic, but the territory would be allowed to display its own flag alongside that of China.

In a toast at the treaty signing in Peking, China's Premier Zhao declared: "We have accomplished a task of historical significance." Britain's Prime Minister Thatcher responded in kind, calling the agreement "a landmark in the life of the territory, in the course of Anglo-Chinese relations, and in the history of international diplomacy." Both were right. The mere fact that Hong Kong would be returning to Chinese sovereignty made the agreement a matter of historical significance. And the unique arrangement by which the transfer would be accomplished made it a landmark of international diplomacy.

For the Communist People's Republic, the accord was also a matter of *ideological* significance. Allowing Hong Kong to keep its capitalist economy was a measure of the remarkable changes taking place in the Chinese way of thinking. The formula of "one nation, two systems" embodied in the agreement bore the unmistakable pragmatic imprint of Deng Xiaoping. In fact, Deng was given credit for the key element in the pact—allowing Hong Kong to remain capitalist for fifty years. It was all a part of China's drive to modernize and open up to Western ways. Shortly after the draft treaty had been initialed in late September, an article in the official party press told the Chinese people not to fear capitalism. "In reality," the article said, "there are many things in capitalism that are useful to socialism."

In Hong Kong, meanwhile, the fear was still very much alive. The agreement had come as a great relief to financial institutions and the general public, but there was lingering concern over the future of the territory. The terms of the transfer were widely acknowledged as the best Hong Kong could have hoped for, but a few key points gave rise to skepticism over Chinese intentions. A major subject of concern was Peking's insistence on a "joint liaison group," composed of five Chinese members and five British, to oversee the transition to Communist rule until the year 2000. The worry in Hong Kong was that the group would be used by Peking as a "shadow government" to undermine Hong Kong's administrative autonomy. Another source of concern was a potential loophole in the agreement by which China could change Hong Kong laws. And most fundamentally, there were fears that Peking might simply ignore the terms of the agreement, or at least some of them. What guarantees were there? What could Britain do if the Chinese went back on their word? What changes might there be in Chinese thinking before 1997? After 1997?

The Hong Kong accord was also a matter of keen interest on the island of Taiwan. The Nationalist leadership reacted to it with alarm, urging the residents of Hong Kong "more vigorously to pursue their struggle against communism for freedom." Among the Taiwanese general public, however, where Peking's reunification proposal does have adherents, Hong Kong would now be viewed as a test of Chinese intentions.

The very best reasons for China to keep its promises on Hong Kong are of course economic. The territory is already China's largest source of foreign exchange. If it is allowed to stay capitalist after 1997, it promises to make even more money for the People's Republic. Nevertheless, there remains great uncertainty over the future of Hong Kong: 1997 is still years away, and the Chinese promises will be tested for another fifty years after that. Given the pace of change in the People's Republic, a half-century could bring several shifts and countershifts in basic policy and ideology. Deng Xiaoping will be gone from the scene even before Hong Kong is officially turned over. Will his pragmatic approach outlive him? For how long? Will subsequent generations of Chinese leaders share his tolerance of capitalism? To what extent? In short, the future of Hong Kong will be the future of China. How it is treated will be a measuring rod of the ongoing changes in the People's Republic.

Chapter 7
Past, Present, and Future

With a recorded history of at least 4,000 years and a cultural heritage that includes magnificent Ming vases, the Great Wall, and the oldest literary tradition in the world, the Chinese have much to look back on with pride. Indeed since the mid-nineteenth century, when Western imperialism first intruded on Chinese autonomy, a central theme in the nation's affairs has been how to make China "rich and strong" again, how to catch up with the West economically, how to reestablish the pride of the Middle Kingdom. From Sun Yat-sen to Chiang Kai-shek, Mao Tse-tung, and Deng Xiaoping, the leaders of the twentieth century have dreamed of restoring China to a position of power and respect among the nations of the world. Three-quarters of the way through the century, however, prosperity and modernization were still unrealized.

Since the death of Mao in 1976, the People's Republic has looked to the future with a new perspective and a new sense of promise. Resisting a deeply entrenched national xenophobia, Deng Xiaoping has opened China to foreign influences as no other leader in the nation's long history. His "pragmatic" policies have set China on a course with distinctly non-Chinese features and an unprecedented reliance on the outside world. In domestic economic policy, the new Peking leadership has implemented basic principles of Western free-market capitalism. In trade and commerce, it has actively sought foreign consumer goods, foreign investment, and the accumulation of foreign exchange. In world policies, it has taken a more active interest in international organizations, exchanged more visits with foreign leaders, and asserted its role in global affairs with greater confidence. And finally, in the spirit of reform, it has allowed deep Western wrinkles in the social and cultural fabric of Chinese life.

These new directions in the Communist revolution nevertheless remain in their infancy. Just how far they will go and just how effective they will be are still to be seen. With all their enthusiasm and all their optimism, the Chinese people express justifiable concern over how long the changes will last. Given all the radical changes in Chinese policy over a mere two generations, another major reversal would come as no great surprise. But even if there were no shift in basic policy or ideology, the reform program will face serious challenges, unforeseen setbacks, and major pitfalls on the long road to prosperity and strength. Both in domestic affairs and on the foreign front, any number of scenarios remains possible.

QUESTIONS
OF APPETITE

With all its overtures to the world at large and all its acceptance of Western ways, the post-Mao leadership has not lost sight of its first priority—to improve the quality of life of the Chinese people. From the earliest stages of Deng's reform program, economic modernization and raising the standard of living have been the guiding considerations in the actual formulation of policy. To the extent that it has developed new trade contacts and increased foreign imports, it has been for the purpose of building a consumer-based economy and filling shortages in basic living needs. To the extent that it has loosened state control and instituted Western-style capitalism, it has been for the purpose of economic efficiency and raising the average family income. And to the extent that it has tolerated Western culture, it has been for the purpose of cultivating a spirit of individual responsibility and reform itself.

Having blamed "radical leftist nonsense" for the lack of economic modernization since 1949, the new Peking leadership has now targeted the mid-twenty-first century as the time when China will catch up with the West. With the interim goal of quadrupling the gross national product by the year 2000, they see the Four Modernizations program making China a major world economic power by the 100th anniversary of the People's Republic.

Perhaps the biggest obstacle to China's economic prosperity is the size of its population, which has severely strained the nation's ability to feed itself and has held back its efforts to modernize. The population figure of one billion is startling in itself, but the greater threat lies in the rate of increase. With Mao Tse-tung declaring "the more people, the better," the post-1949 era saw a major baby boom; consequently, about 65 percent of China's population today is under 30, many of them just reaching childbearing age. To cope with another impending boom, Chinese officials instituted tough family-planning measures in 1979. Married couples in China today are allowed to have only one child. Those who pledge to have just one are given work bonuses, priorities in housing and education, and other special privileges; those who refuse

A billboard in Peking promoting China's one family, one child policy. "WO" means "One."

forfeit a portion of their wages, lose benefits and raises, and come under intense pressure from local officials. In addition, community birth-control monitoring, abortions, and sterilization procedures have been stepped up. Peking's official goal is a population of 1.2 billion by the year 2000.

Hand in hand with the population problem is the growing problem of unemployment. Under the old "Iron rice bowl" system, virtually every worker had guaranteed employment in a state-run factory. With industrial plants now being run on a competitive-market basis, more streamlined work crews yield greater profits. As fewer and fewer workers are being hired, the rate of unemployment is beginning to catch up with the rate of economic growth.

Another danger to Peking's economic reform program is inflation. With its emphasis on light industry and consumer goods, the new approach has triggered a strong Chinese appetite for appliances and other items once considered luxuries. While the regime continues to build an economy driven by consumption rather than production, unchecked free spending on the part of the Chinese masses will send prices skyrocketing and strangle economic growth.

In a similar vein, the new economic growth has whetted an appetite for profits so keen that the means of production are being dangerously neglected. In the industrial sector, the furious pursuit of profits has left some machinery poorly maintained. In some rural areas, the land has not been adequately tended; overcultivation has caused a growing problem of land erosion.

The biggest question marks, however, are the unanticipated developments that neither Peking nor the Chinese people can control. Can the new economic system survive a string of bad crops? A major downturn in the world economy? What if the South China

Sea does not yield as much oil as expected? Can industrial growth and development be sustained without it? And finally, will the next generation of Chinese economic planners endure the challenges? Or will they have lost their appetite for capitalism, consumerism, and class distinctions?

BONDS

The People's Republic of China has played a unique role—and faced unique pressures—in the arena of international politics. As a nuclear power and the world's most populous nation, it carries enormous military and economic potential. For that reason alone its alignment within the "strategic triangle" can tilt the balance of world power toward either the United States or the Soviet Union. As a nation that is still developing and not a superpower in its own right, however, it must look to the outside for its basic security. At the same time, like the Third World countries with which it now identifies, China seeks to maintain its autonomy and "nonalignment" in the international community.

During the 1980s, the People's Republic has struck a delicate balance. While declaring an "independent foreign policy" and developing new ties with the Third World, it maintains a shared strategic interest with the United States in opposing the Soviet Union. This dual position is made possible in large measure by the aggressive attitude being taken toward Moscow by the U.S. administration of Ronald Reagan. With the Soviets held in check by Washington, Peking has been free to ease its own tensions with Moscow.

In the long term, this somewhat negative bond between China and the United States—opposition to the Soviets—may prove tenuous. Were U.S.-Soviet relations to enter a period of détente and arms reduction, China would be forced to fend more for itself in opposing the Soviets. Were U.S.-Soviet tensions to heighten, China might feel freer to stray from the Washington line. And ultimately, if China itself develops into a major economic and military power, its reliance on Washington will decline measurably.

Both for China and the West, however, there is now an opening for a more positive, long-term bond. The liberal trend within China and the need for Western participation in its modernization efforts offer the hope of a partnership strong enough to absorb basic differences (as over Taiwan). Indeed China's drive for modernization at home remains the key to its policies abroad. Were the reform program to be abandoned, the international implications might be serious. Ideologically and economically at odds with the West, China might speed up its takeover of Hong Kong and make aggressive moves against Taiwan. That would create confrontations with Great Britain and the United States. A return to Marxism-Leninism might also revive China's interest in promoting national revolutions in Asia and Africa.

As long as Deng's reform program remains alive, however, it will be in China's strong interest to promote peace and stability abroad. It will continue its open-door policy with the West and continue to develop strong trade and cultural ties with the Western democracies. It will retain its liberal position toward Hong Kong and Taiwan. And it will continue to seek new partners in Asia and the Pacific. This new internationalism will help develop a peaceful environment for domestic growth—and provide valuable economic benefits.

The swings in Chinese foreign policy over past decades reflect a way of thinking that goes back to the ancient emperors and was put into words by Mao

Tse-tung: "Let foreign things serve China." Future directions appear likely to be determined by the same philosophy.

THREE CHINAS

During the first decades of Mao Tse-tung's regime, Westerners looking at the People's Republic (usually from the outside) often asked: Is China more Chinese or more Communist? For despite Mao's radical new ethic and all his efforts to subdue old values, China still clung to many of its ancient traditions and institutions; 4,000 years do not die so easily. Now, after all the changes that have taken place since Mao's death, the question is beng reformulated: Is China more Chinese, more Communist, or more Western?

That third aspect—the ways in which China has adopted elements of Western thinking and culture—remains the most unsettled part of China's present identity, and also the most rapidly developing. The spirit of radical Maoist Communism appears to have been put to rest, though the current regime does retain its basic socialist outlook. And while the Mao and Deng regimes both have challenged some traditional values and cultural institutions, life in China still has strong ties with the past. Interestingly, the reforms being implemented by Peking's new pragmatic leaders emphasize many of the same values as traditional Confucianism: hard work, respect for the learned, and ethical responsibility.

Thus, in interesting and ever-changing ways, the People's Republic today reflects the character of three different Chinas: the proud, ancient China of cultural splendor, imperial sovereignty, and the Great Wall; Mao's China of collectivization, the Red Guard, and the "bamboo curtain"; and Deng's China of "household responsibility," the open-door policy, and the Great Wall Hotel. The enigmas, uncertainties, and ever-shifting policies of the modern People's Republic reflect the competing forces of these three Chinas. Whatever shape the Chinese character finally takes, it will be a unique mixture of these three cultural and historical influences.

In looking toward the twenty-first century, Deng Xiaoping has told the world that "our present line, principles, policies, and strategies will not change." But despite his best efforts to ensure that post-Deng China will continue to pursue pragmatic reform, there are no guarantees. The course of Chinese policy may not be bound to Deng's legacy any more than it was bound to Mao's. Neither will Washington or Moscow dictate the course of Peking policy. The Chinese nation is so vast, its problems so unique, and its temperament so fiercely independent that subsequent generations will forge their *own* path, step by step, forward to modernization and back to the Middle Kingdom.

The fascination of China's past is exceeded only by the fascination of its future.

For Further
Reading

The changes taking place inside the People's Republic of China have been richly chronicled in several recent books. Orville Schell's *To Get Rich Is Glorious: China in the 1980's* (Pantheon Books, 1984) and *"Watch Out for the Foreign Guests!"* (Pantheon Books, 1980) give vivid accounts and revealing observations on the transformation of modern China. In *China: Alive in the Bitter Sea* (Times Books, 1982), newspaper journalist Fox Butterfield draws a fascinating, in-depth portrait of life in the contemporary People's Republic. And China's rich history and cultural tradition are brought to bear in *China: Yesterday and Today*, by Molly Joel Coye and Jon Livingston (Bantam Books, 1984), and in *The Heart of the Dragon*, by Alasdair Clayre (Houghton Mifflin, 1984).

Given the pace of change, however, it is especially useful to follow the course of events in your daily newspaper or favorite news magazine. Western journalists reporting directly from the People's Republic are giving insightful accounts of the ongoing developments in politics, economy, foreign affairs, and day-to-day life. *Current History*, a monthly journal of world affairs, provides in-depth analyses of several key domestic and foreign policy issues in its yearly edition on the People's Republic (usually issued in September).

For a historical perspective, John K. Fairbank's *The United States and China* (Harvard University Press, 1979) is the classic introduction to China for general audiences. Edgar Snow's *Red Star Over China* (Grove Press, 1961) is another classic: this tells of the life of Mao Tse-tung and the growth of the Communist movement in China. Yuan-Tsung Chen's *The Dragon's Village* (Pantheon, 1980) covers the revolution and the dilemma of land reform in a village as conducted by urban youth. *China: U.S. Policy Since 1945*, published by Congressional Quarterly, Inc., is a valuable source book for the years up to 1980. Liang Heng and Judith Shapiro's *Son of the Revolution* (Knopf, 1983) covers the late 1950s through the Cultural Revolution. Ross Terrill's *The Future of China After Mao* (Delacorte Press, 1978) focuses on the critical years of 1976 and 1977, setting the stage for the emergence of the "New China." And books on virtually any other aspect of Chinese history, culture, and politics can be found on the shelves of any school or public library.

Index